S0-AIS-130

PROCEEDINGS OF THE NATIONAL CONFERENCE

FUTURE FRONTIERS

IN THE EMPLOYMENT OF MINORITY PERSONS WITH DISABILITIES

Edited by

Sylvia Walker

Faye Z. Belgrave

Robert W. Nicholls

Kimberley A. Turner

Co-sponsored by
THE PRESIDENT'S COMMITTEE ON EMPLOYMENT OF PEOPLE WITH DISABILITIES
and
HOWARD UNIVERSITY RESEARCH AND TRAINING CENTER
FOR ACCESS TO REHABILITATION AND ECONOMIC OPPORTUNITY

1991

Proceedings of the 1990 National Conference "Future frontiers in the employment of minority persons with disabilities," March 28-30, 1990

In addition to the support received from the President's Committee on Employment of People with Disabilities, this publication was supported in part by a grant from the U.S. Department of Education, National Institute on Disability and Rehabilitation Research, Grant Number H133B80059. The opinions expressed herein are those of the authors and should not be attributed to the U.S. Department of Education or the co-sponsors.

Copies of this monograph can be obtained by writing to:

Dr. Sylvia Walker, Director
Howard University Research and Training Center for
 Access to Rehabilitation and Economic Opportunity
2900 Van Ness Street, N.W.
Holy Cross Hall, Suite 100
Washington, D.C. 20008

or,

Mr. Claude Grant, Jr., Program Manager
President's Committee on Employment of People with Disabilities
1331 F Street, N.W.
Washington, D.C. 20004-1107

CONTENTS

SECTION I: POLICY IMPLICATIONS AND FUTURE FORECASTS

SECTION II: NEW FRONTIERS IN MULTICULTURAL APPROACHES

SECTION III: FRONTIERS IN ASSISTIVE TECHNOLOGY

PREFACE

RICHARD DOUGLAS
EXECUTIVE DIRECTOR
PRESIDENT'S COMMITTEE ON EMPLOYMENT
OF PEOPLE WITH DISABILITIES

As the new Executive Director of the President's Committee on Employment of People with Disabilities, I am pleased to offer these comments. The Conference reported in this publication focused on national issues relative to the employment of minority persons with disabilities. Their high unemployment rate, documented in the 1980 Census, is startling. The incidence of disability among African Americans and Hispanics is much higher than that of their White peers. As a result of the 1980 Census Bureau Report, the 1987 National Conference was formed and subsequent regional minority conference meetings were conducted to address the grave employment crisis faced by African Americans with disabilities.

Since the 1987 National Conference, much attention has been given to the plight of other minority persons with disabilities. The 1980 Census data pointed out that one working age adult in seven has a disability. Of 16,157,000 African American adults age 16 to 64 and not in institutions, 14.1% have disabilities. There are 2,280,000 African American adults with disabilities. The report revealed that one working age Hispanic adult in twelve has a disability. Of 8,325,000 Hispanic adults between the ages of 16 and 64 who are not in institutions, 702,000 or 8.4% have a disability.

These findings are a real challenge to government and private industry to bring more minority individuals with disabilities into the labor market. This conference addressed some of the employment issues and problems relevant to Asian/Pacific Americans and Native Americans with disabilities. Within the last few years attention has been given to the employment dilemma faced by Asian/Pacific Americans and Native Americans with disabilities. Asian/Pacific Americans and Native Americans comprise a small percentage of the American population, however, it is believed that both groups have high incidences of disability. Further, it is believed that the unemployment rate for both groups of persons with disabilities is extremely high. Minority persons with disabilities should be considered and selected for gainful and meaningful employment. Also, they should be recruited and selected for positions that will provide for upward mobility. The goal of the National

Conference was to continue to explore means of eliminating and reducing existing barriers to employment, educational opportunities, and rehabilitative services. Methods for facilitating employment opportunities for these individuals need to be identified.

The presentations were excellent and clearly outlined the needs of minority persons with disabilities. The following topics were discussed: increased rehabilitative services, better educational opportunities, forming partnerships and linkages, leadership development, mentoring, etc. A common thread that ran throughout the National Conference was that minority persons with disabilities are underserved and that there has been no real effort by the service delivery systems to correct the problems.

We are deeply appreciative of the hard work that was done by the organizers and planners of this much needed conference. Special thanks are extended to Dr. Sylvia Walker for spearheading this conference.

We are grateful to each panelist for sharing their precious thoughts and ideas about the various topics which they discussed. It is my hope that each of us have gained some valuable information from this worthwhile conference and that this conference will motivate each of us to do our part in assisting minority persons with disabilities in securing gainful employment. Gainful employment for minority persons with disabilities will greatly aid in obtaining economic independence.

ACKNOWLEDGEMENTS

The editors would like to extend their warmest and sincerest appreciation to each of the contributors and to the many national and local rehabilitation, medical, educational, technological, and other service delivery agencies who contributed to the success of the Conference and the publication of these proceedings.

We are grateful to those individuals who worked very hard in the preparation of this publication. Special thanks are given to Mr. George Covington, Special Assistant to Vice-President Dan Quayle and Mr. Claudie Grant of the President's Committee on the Employment of People with Disabilities for their support; and to Ms. Marilyn D. Miles, Ms. Anntoinette McFadden, Mrs. Ada Vincent, Ms. Tremetrice Houston, and Ms. Elaine Vinson for their outstanding editorial assistance. We are especially appreciative of the support which we have received from the School of Education at Howard University, the National Institute of Disability and Rehabilitation Research (of the U.S. Department of Education), the President's Committee on the Employment of People with Disabilities, members of the National Advisory Committee, and the corporate sector including Digital Equipment Corp., AT&T, IBM, and New Jersey Bell.

Finally, the cooperation and collaboration rendered by administrators, staff, students, and faculty of various institutions and organizations facilitated the accomplishment of the identified objectives providing a stimulating and informative conference in an atmosphere of fellowship and the subsequent publication and dissemination of the conference proceedings.

This publication is dedicated
to the memory of
Eula Mae Walker Thomas
of the City of New York

Mrs. Thomas (Dr. Sylvia Walker's mother)
was committed to making the American Dream
a reality for all.

FUTURE FRONTIERS

POLICY IMPLICATIONS AND FUTURE FORECASTS

FUTURE FRONTIERS IN THE EMPLOYMENT
OF MINORITY PERSONS WITH DISABILITIES:
NIDRR'S ROLE

WILLIAM H. GRAVES, DIRECTOR
NIDRR

Abstract

Some thirty-three million Americans have a disability and a large percent of these are members of minority groups. The purpose of NIDRR is to promote and coordinate research related to individuals with disabilities. This is accomplished through NIDRR's discretionary grant program. NIDRR works collaboratively with organizations such as Howard University to meet the needs of minority individuals with disabilities.

Over the past 25 years, the prevalence of severe disability has increased 70 percent. During the next 20 years, we can expect further increases as the baby boom generation enters middle age, when the risk of acquiring disability jumps sharply. Today, some 33 million Americans have a disability. If current trends continue, the number of Americans with disabilities will reach 41 million by the year 2000 and 47 million by 2010. Of these numbers, we can expect a large percentage to be members of minority groups. A large percentage--as great as 60 percent-- of individuals with disabilities have work-related disabilities. The 1986 Louis Harris survey of disabled adults stated, "Not working is perhaps the truest definition of what it means to be disabled in this country." Of the 20 million working-age Americans that are work-disabled, 13 million are jobless.

NIDRR was established by the Rehabilitation Act Amendments in 1978. Its purpose is to promote and coordinate research related to individuals with disabilities. It achieves this purpose through its discretionary grant programs. Currently, NIDRR has a 74.1 million dollar budget. This amount includes the basic NIDRR appropriation ($54.3 million), spinal cord injury projects ($5.0 million), state grants for technology assistance ($12.5 million), and projects of national significance ($2.3 million). Out of these funds, 11 discretionary grant programs are funded. These grant programs include research and demonstration projects, Rehabilitation Research and Training Centers, innovation grants, dissemination and utilization projects, REC's, fellowships, field initiated, research training, spinal cord injury, tech act, and projects of national significance. What does this have to do with my topic? Everything.

The mission of NIDRR is to promote research activities which provide a foundation for individuals with disabilities and for educational and rehabilitation service providers to meet their needs today and in the future. Whether or not NIDRR is successful in building and maintaining this foundation depends in no small part on NIDRR's collaboration with groups, individuals, and organizations interested in people with disabilities. NIDRR intends to work with its grantees, such as Howard University, to build and maintain the foundation that supports the efforts of individuals with disabilities and of educational and rehabilitation service providers.

NIDRR intends to work collaboratively with organizations relevant to its mission. This work, if it is to meet the future needs of minority individuals with disabilities, must be true collaboration, not what Richard Parson, the 18th century British classicist noted when asked by a junior scholar to collaborate on a work -- "It's a wonderful idea! Put in all I know and all you know, and it will make a great work!" How will NIDRR collaborate in order to meet these future needs? (1) Maximizing opportunities for input, advice, and consultation from and with NIDRR's target population, (2) Peer Review, (3) RFP's proposed priorities, (4) Visits to NIDRR, and (5) Serving on task forces. One of my goals as Director of NIDRR is to assist in increasing the number of rehabilitation researchers who have disabilities. Increasing the supply of rehabilitation researchers will increase the likelihood of NIDRR building a foundation for meeting the future frontiers in the employment of minority persons with disabilities.

Thank you for the opportunity to be with you at this conference. I look forward to working with you in the months ahead.

STATUS OF MINORITY PERSONS WITH DISABILITIES:
WHERE DO WE GO FROM HERE:

HOWARD MOSES
EQUAL EMPLOYMENT OPPORTUNITIES COMMISSION*

Abstract

This article highlights statistics on unemployment rates and income levels by gender and age among Hispanics and African Americans with disabilities. The author compares 1980 and 1988 statistics with regard to employment rates and income levels for persons with disabilities and the non-disabled. The article also includes a number of recommendations which were the results of hearings held by Commissioner Carney.

I must say that Justin Dart has been a key individual in my life during the last five years. He talked about patience and perseverance. When I came to Washington, DC to work for Justin, these were not my top qualities. Believe me, Justin's ability to exhibit kindness, love, and patience is an example from which I have learned. It is only through his leadership that I have been able to accomplish what I have in the disability movement. I am deeply indebted to this man for who and what I am today.

On a lighter note, when an individual is asked to speak to groups, there are certain obligations which one must adhere to. The first obligation, I am told, is that the speaker is responsible for telling a joke. So, I will tell a joke. There was an elderly man who had a grandfather clock which had been in his family for decades. He loved this clock very much. Unfortunately, the clock stopped working one morning. The elderly man was upset. He was able to find a repair shop that was open. The clock repair man came, picked up the clock, and took it to the shop. As usual, it took about six weeks to complete the repairs; but finally, the clock repair man called and told the man that his clock was ready. The man was absolutely thrilled. He felt that his life had been almost lost without his clock in the house. However, he could not find anybody to bring it back to his house, so he decided that he was going to carry his clock home by himself. Upon arriving at the shop, he decided that the best way to carry the clock would be to put it on his back and carry it down the street.

*Former Special Assistant to the Commissioner, Rehabilitation Services Administration

As he was doing this, he happened to pass a local drinking establishment, from which a lightly inebriated individual walked out the door, lunged into the old man, and knocked the clock off his back. The clock fell and broke into a thousand pieces. Picking himself up, the old man said, "why don't you watch where you are going?" The drunk responded, "why don't you get a wrist watch?"

That story does not relate too well to what we are talking about here today, but there is another story that addresses our topic -- the story of two campers who were out in the wilds of the Arctic north. One night, as they were sitting around their camp fire, they heard a bear coming down upon the camp. As it become obvious that the bear was getting very close, one of the campers began to put on his snow shoes. The other individual asked, "what are you doing putting on your snow shoes? You can't outrun that bear." The first camper responded, "I don't have to outrun the bear, I only have to outrun you." Unfortunately, that story does have a moral for what we are talking about. In this day of limited resources and budgets, far too many of us find ourselves in that foot race where each person tries not to be the one that the bear gobbles first. Individuals with disabilities, especially those from minority groups, are definitely in that foot race everyday.

One other obligation of speaking on a college campus is that one has to cite statistics in order to show some type of scholarly approach with regard to what one is saying. Therefore, I am going to cite some statistics from the Census Bureau. I love the way the Census Bureau puts things, so I am going to read them verbatim. In referring to Hispanics with disabilities, it said, and I quote, "most Hispanics with disabilities of working age are neither working or looking for work. They are not in the labor force." (Bowe, 1983)

In March of 1982, unemployment among women stood at 21.8%, and for that same month, the percentage for men, 24.2% Overall, 23.3% of working age Hispanics with disabilities were unemployed. An analysis of 1980 Census Bureau data revealed that three in ten Hispanics with disabilities of working age report income from all sources of under $2,000 per year. In addition, one in four Hispanics with a disability had an income between the levels of $2,000 and $3,999 per year. By contrast, only 17% reported an income over $8,000 per year. Census data from 1982 relative to African Americans with disabilities indicated that labor force participation was very limited since most persons in this category were neither working nor seeking work. Fewer than one in four was either working or seeking work. Of those in the labor force, slightly more than one quarter were not

5

working, but seeking work. Income and economic status for African Americans with disabilities were also bleak. Almost one third reported income from all sources of less than $2,000 and $4,000 annually.

I do not have any overall data for minority groups for the period 1982-1988, however, I do have some data for populations with disabilities for the year 1988. They are as follow: the percentage of men with a work-disability, working full time, fell from 30% in 1981 to 23% in 1988. During the same time period, the income of workers with disabilities dropped sharply compared with that of other workers. In 1980, men with disabilities earned 23% less than men with no work disability (Bowe, 1983); and by 1988, this discrepancy increased since in 1988 they were earning 36% less than their non-disabled counterparts. In 1980, women with disabilities earned 30% less than women without disabilities. By 1988, the percentage income earned by the latter was 38% less than it was for their non-disabled counterparts. There are sharp differences in income levels for minority groups as compared to the general population. Research conducted for the National Council on Disability revealed that minority groups with disabilities fared even worse than their White counterparts during the 1980's (National Council on Disability, 1990).

It is obvious that persons with disabilities lost ground during a period of economic up-turn and a period that was the longest post-war period of economic growth. Both workers with disabilities and non-workers with disabilities lost ground during the decade of the 80's. I am not a betting man, I do not bet on very many things, nor do I participate in the lottery, but I would be willing to make a bet that two years hence, someone will be standing on this stage talking to a population very similar to you, saying that the 1990 census results, which are being collected right now, reflect a worse situation, and I doubt that I would lose my money on that bet.

For rehabilitation, minority groups with disabilities pose a number of unique problems. Very few statistics for rehabilitation of individuals of Hispanic origin exist. Most estimates for Hispanics with disabilities total about 2.5 million. In 1981, there were only 25,000 persons of Hispanic origin who were rehabilitated by state agencies. None of this is to reflect upon the work of state agencies across this nation, nor is it to reflect upon the work of individual vocational rehabilitation counselors. However, it does reflect upon the problems that we have in the rehabilitation field.

6

What do we do about it? (That is the nice thing about being an early speaker at a conference: You can ask that question and be certain that nobody has answered it before you ask it). Justin has already pointed out that the first thing we must do is pass the Americans with Disabilities Act. Some very specific things that we can do have been pointed out to Rehabilitation Services Administration Commissioner Carney through her travels around the country. The Commissioner fulfilled her commitment that she would attend constituencies meetings in all ten federal regions. During those meetings, she met with Native Americans and representatives from Section 130 Indian Programs (which were funded by the Rehabilitation Services Administration). She has also met with Hispanic groups and with other minority groups in various parts of the country. The following are among the recommendations which were made by various groups during the hearings held by Commissioner Carney:

1. Build a better service delivery system for minority persons with disabilities by being aggressive in the recruitment and training of rehabilitation professionals from the minority community.

2. Establish cross-cultural training for rehabilitation personnel to sensitize them to the special concerns and needs of the minority populations with disabilities.

3. Require all universities to include the course titled, "Rehabilitation in a Pluralistic Society," in their curricula for rehabilitation counselors.

4. Have training grants to fund rehabilitation aide positions recruited from minority communities to assist the rehabilitation counselors in bridging the gap between the rehabilitation agency and consumers with disabilities.

5. Develop outreach programs.

6. Give consideration to the needs of minority individuals with disabilities when developing policy for rehabilitation agencies and independent living centers.

The above recommendations will increase access to rehabilitation services by persons with disabilities. I could go on and on, but these specific items highlight the suggestions received by the Commissioner from individuals across the country. However, I would like to leave you with a larger perspective that gives you some framework which can be useful for the rest of the conference. My major concern at this point, is the lack of minorities with disabilities in key management positions responsible for disability policy. Whenever I start talking about the larger perspective, I always hesitate and think about several concerns which are clearly represented in a book written by a young man who is a quadriplegic and a cartoonist from the state of Washington. (The theme of the book, <u>Don't Worry, You won't be Fired for This</u>, is overcoming his disability as well as his own alcoholism). When talking about the larger perspective, I am forced to think about that title sometimes. The first thing that needs to occur at the national level is the appointment of Hispanics, African Americans, and other minority individuals with disabilities to key management positions responsible for disability policy. We have seen some movement in that direction with the appointment of Dr. Davilla, Assistant Secretary for Special Education and Rehabilitation Services within the Department of Education. I can also point to my friend, Diedre Davis, who served as Director of the Independent Living Program within the Rehabilitation Services Administration. However, two people in those positions is not enough.

Another aspect of the overall perspective which we need to look at very seriously is the economic and social policy context in which our current rehabilitation practices are being conducted. Can our rehabilitation strategies work within the limits of social policies and economic conditions? I will just give you some examples of some things that we need to consider. People with disabilities learned a long time ago what happens when they are not there when decisions are made. We can ask ourselves the following questions: What good is a successful Project with Industry (PWI) strategy on an Indian reservation that has no industry? What good is an urban center for independent living that can give you information on English as a Second Language in large print or braille, but has no one on staff who speaks Spanish? In many cases, cultural barriers can be just as burdensome as architectural barriers. We have to recognize that our partnership at the federal level must be as strong with the Department of Commerce as it has been with the Department of Labor in our job training and job development efforts. Our ability to place individuals with disabilities in employment in inner cities has more to do with policies affecting red-lining in the banking industry than our ability to provide rehabilitation technology. Our ability to place individuals with disabilities in employment on Indian reservations, many times, has more to do with the development of capital, or the accumulation of capital and the policies of Fannie Mae than do our strategies in providing rehabilitation services in rural settings.

Until the Office of Management and Budget, the White House, and the Congress begin to think of disability policy in the context of economic development, the census figures that we will see in the year 2000 will be no better than the census figures I quoted to you earlier for 1980 and 1988.

The final obligation of a speaker is to quit while he is ahead. So I am going to turn it over from here and hope I gave you some food for thought. I wish you well with the conference. The Commissioner sends her regards. If there is anything that we can do through the Rehabilitation Services Administration to assist in implementing the findings of the conference, we welcome that input. Thank you!

References

Bowe, F. (1983) Demography and disability: A chartbook for rehabilitation. Arkansas Rehabilitation Research and Training Center. Little Rock: University of Arkansas, Arkansas Rehabilitation Services.

National Council on Disability (1990, November) Writing National Policy on Work Disability. (Program Prospectus). Washington, DC

PREVALENCE, DISTRIBUTION AND IMPACT OF DISABILITY AMONG ETHNIC MINORITIES

SYLVIA WALKER, CHARLES ASBURY,
VALERIE MAHOLMES, AND REGINALD RACKLEY,
HOWARD UNIVERSITY RESEARCH AND TRAINING CENTER

Abstract

This paper begins by noting the factors contributing to high minority disability rates. The objectives of this study were to gather data on disability rates of major ethnic minority groups in the U.S.; to gather information on the geographic distribution of ethnic minorities with disabilities; to gather data on specific types of disabilities, and to gather demographic data on the age, sex, employment and marital status of these persons. Prevalence data for focus groups and reference variables were presented. Focal group variables were chronic debilitating health conditions, physical impairments, limitations of activity, mental disorders, and nervous conditions. Reference group variables were race, age, sex, education, income, marital status and metropolitan statistical area. The impact of these various conditions on the lives of individuals with these conditions are discussed. The findings of this study are essential to understanding disability prevalence of ethnic minorities and should guide policy in this area.

INTRODUCTION

There is currently a dearth of comprehensive information available on the prevalence of specific types of disabilities among ethnic minorities groups such as African Americans, Hispanics, Native Americans and Asian/Pacific Islanders. Consensus based on available global evidence suggests that disability is much more prevalent in minority than non-minority populations (Bowe, 1985a, 1985b; Thornhill and HoSang, 1988; Walker, Akpati, Roberts, Palmer, and Newsome, 1988).

Among the factors that have been suggested as contributing to higher minority disability rates are poor prenatal and perinatal care, nutrition and diet, greater risk for physical injury because of living conditions and types of employment situations, an inaccessible health care system and finally lack of proper health care knowledge and education (Walker, 1987). In order to arrest the cycle of inappropriate and insufficient health care and education contributing to disability, programs and policies must be developed to meet the needs of individuals who are most at risk. The information provided through this study on the prevalence, distribution, and impact of disability among ethnic minorities can serve as a basis for developing these policies and educational initiatives.

10

The objectives of this research study, therefore, were to gather prevalence data on the disability rates of major ethnic minority groups in the U.S.; to gather information on the geographic distribution of ethnic minorities with disabilities; to gather prevalence data on specific types of disabilities characteristic of these ethnic minorities and lastly, to gather demographic data on the age, sex, employment, and marital status of these persons.

Variables

In this study, one set of variables was labelled, "Focal Group Variables" and the other, "Reference Variables." The focal group variables were chronic debilitating health conditions, physical impairments, limitations of activity (LOA), mental disorders and nervous conditions. The reference variables were age, sex, education, income, employment, marital status, metropolitan statistical area, and race.

The focal group variables were further sub-divided to include: chronic conditions, impairments, limitation of activity, mental disorders and nervous conditions. The chronic conditions were: invertebral disc disorders, diabetes, high blood pressure and arthritis. The impairments were: hearing, orthopedic, visual, paralysis of extremities, absence of extremities and speech disorder. Two types of limitations of activity, functional and work activity, were investigated. The four category levels for functional LOA were: no activity limitation, limited, but not in major activity; limited in major activity, and unable to carry on major activity. The four category levels for working LOA were: no activity limitation; limited, but not in major activity; limited in other activities; and unable to work. Mental disorders were: schizophrenia, affective psychoses, and other psychoses. Categories for nervous conditions were mental retardation, cerebral palsy, Parkinson Disease, epilepsy, multiple sclerosis, and other disorders (including Alzheimer's disease).

The reference variables were subdivided to include different categories (levels and ranges) for particular variables. For example, the range for "age" is from under six years to 75 years and over. The range for variable "income" is from under $5,000 per year through $50,000 or more per year. Metropolitan statistical area ranges are from 100,000 to 1,000,000 or more people. Marital status includes the categories married, spouse at home; married, spouse not at home; widowed; divorced; separated, and never married. Employment was divided into those currently "employed," "unemployed," and "not in the labor force." Race was categorized as White, Black, Hispanic and other; while Gender was categorized as male and female.

DESIGN AND METHODOLOGY

The primary data source is the National Health Survey used to generate data for the National Center for Health Statistics (NCHS). In keeping with the purpose of the study, two data tapes which cover a broad range of demographic and health related factors were secured from the NCHS. When completely analyzed, the recently secured 1987 data tape will yield the latest information regarding prevalence and distribution of disabilities and will also enable us to examine trends for associating focal group variables with reference variables over a specified period of time. The present report is based primarily on a 1986 data tape. Where applicable, however, reference will be made to the more current information of the 1987 tape.

The sample for this study consists of 62,052 persons from 23,838 households interviewed in 1986. The target population was the resident, civilian, noninstitutionalized population residing in the United States. Essentially, the sampling procedure was multi-stage and based on primary sampling units selected in such a way as to insure accurate representativeness.

At this point, the preliminary findings for chronic conditions, physical impairments, mental disorders, nervous conditions and limitations of activity will be briefly discussed. In keeping with the theme of this conference, the prevalence and incidence of those conditions which have the most deleterious impact upon the income and employment status of ethnic minorities will be highlighted.

RESULTS

Chronic Conditions

For the total group of chronic conditions subjects, the three most prevalent conditions were arthritis (26.2%), high blood pressure (21.2%), and heart disease (19.5%) with two-thirds of the chronic conditions sample having one of these conditions.

12

The findings indicate that when examined by race, the absolute number of chronic conditions were found to be more prevalent among Whites. Of the total population reporting these conditions, 80.6% were White, 12.6% were Black and 5.3% were Hispanic. However, there was considerable variation in the rates among ethnic groups for specific types of conditions.

The trend for associating the highest rates of specific chronic health conditions according to race appeared to be heart disease (White), arthritis (White), high blood pressure (Black), respiratory disorder (Hispanic), diabetes (Hispanic), invertebrate disc disorder (White), and cerebrovascular disease (Black).

A comparison of disability rates across age categories shows a trend for the prevalence of chronic health conditions to increase with age. This trend was generally observed across all age categories with fewer young people having these conditions, but with a steady increase as people get older.

The majority of the persons in the chronic conditions sample were not in the labor force (65.7%). Thirty one point nine percent were employed and 2.5% were unemployed. The most prevalent chronic conditions among the employed were high blood pressure (25.4%), arthritis (23.3%) and respiratory disorders (16.7%). Among the unemployed, the most prevalent conditions were arthritis (27%) and respiratory disorders (19.5%) with high blood pressure (18.7%) and heart disease (18.3%) very close in prevalence. The most prevalent condition among persons not in the labor force was arthritis (29.9%).

Finally, on the basis on income, findings show that the most prevalent conditions for persons earning between $7,000 - 9,999 per year were arthritis (30%) high blood pressure (20.7%) and heart disease (19.6%). In the $15,000 - 19,000 income group, the most prevalent conditions were arthritis (27%), heart disease (20.8%), and high blood pressure (19.8%). The most prevalent conditions in the $25,000 - 34,999 income range were arthritis (21.7%), high blood pressure (21.4%), and respiratory disorder (20.4%). The pattern for prevalence of chronic conditions for persons earning $50,000 or more was arthritis (23.1%), respiratory disorder (22.5%) and high blood pressure (18.5%).

Impairments

For the total group of physically impaired subjects, the three most prevalent conditions were orthopedic impairments(57%), hearing impairments (19.5%), and visual impairments (11.6%) with slightly over two-thirds of the physical impairments sample having one of these conditions. These results suggest an order for focusing attention and prioritizing policies.

Preliminary results of impairments show that the most prominent type was orthopedic with 57% of all impaired subjects in this group. Examination of the highest incidence of particular impairments across races shows that 85.4% of the hearing impaired were White, 16.6% of the speech impaired were Black, and 6.5% of the orthopedically impaired subjects were Hispanic. These impairments were the ones showing the highest percentages according to the ethnic groups indicated.

Over 86% of all persons with a physical impairment were over the age of 24. The general tendency seems to be that physical impairment also increases with age. An exception to this was seen for speech impairment with higher prevalence rates, for the most part, in the age 17 and under group. Across all categories, a higher incidence of impairments found in the 6-16 year age group was speech impairment, the 65-74 age group was absence of extremities, the over 74 age group was visual and hearing, and the 35-44 age group was orthopedic.

Among employed persons, the most prevalent impairments were orthopedic (68.3%), hearing (17.2%) and visual (8.7%). This means that the impaired persons most likely to be employed are orthopedically impaired, hearing impaired, and visually impaired. Among those not in the labor force, the most prevalent impairments were orthopedic (49.2%) and hearing impairment (21.4%). Unemployment rates were generally highest for people with orthopedic (63.3%), hearing (16.3%) and visual (11.5%) impairments.

An examination by income showed that for persons earning between $7,000 - 9,999 and $50,000 or more, orthopedic, hearing and visual were the most prevalent impairments. The highest prevalence rates of physical impairment were found primarily in the $7,000 - 9,999 category. The following impairments were represented in this income category: hearing, (25.5%), orthopedic (26.4%), visual (29.6%), paralysis (38.9%) loss of extremities (23%) and speech (31.2%). Although deviations for the 1987 sample were not substantial, a moderate increase from 28.9% to 37.5% was found for paralysis.

Limitation of Activity (Functional)

Approximately 35.3% of the chronic conditions sample and 37% of the total impairment sample had no activity limitations. The largest percentage among categories of limited activity in the chronic conditions sample was 23.4% for "limited in kind or amount of major activity." The same was true in the impairment sample where 24% were limited in the kind or amount of major activity. The highest percentage of functional LOA among persons with chronic conditions was observed for cerebrovascular disease where 51.3% were unable to perform major activities. This value was lowered somewhat (47.8), however, when reported for the 1987 sample. Of the persons with impairments the highest percentages in the not limited category were found among subjects with hearing impairments. This contrasts sharply with paralysis subjects, where 51% were unable to perform major activities.

Limitations of Activity (Work)

Approximately 35.1% of the chronic conditions sample had no activity limitations, while 39.1% of the impairments sample also reported having no activity limitation. Moreover, among persons with chronic health conditions, another 34.5% reported that they were unable to work, and of the total sample, 18.9% indicated that there was a limitation in the kind or amount of work they could do.

The highest prevalence rates among chronic condition subjects was for cerebrovascular disease with 71.7% reporting that they were unable to work. In the impairment groups, the highest prevalence was for the paralysis subjects with 64.6% reporting that they were unable to work. With minor deviations, this picture was also observed for the 1987 sample. Fewer stroke patients reported inability to work and a slightly larger number of people with paralysis reported inability to work.

Mental Disorders

For the total group of subjects with mental disorders, schizophrenia (38.2%) was the most prevalent, followed by other psychoses (35.6%) and affective psychoses (26.2%). When the data were analyzed by race, it was clear that White subjects were approximately equally distributed across the three disorder categories, schizophrenia (34.4%), affective psychoses (32.7%) and other psychoses (32.8%). In contrast, Blacks were not so evenly spread. More than one-half (56.5%) had schizophrenia, 40.9% had other psychoses and a minimal number had affective psychoses (2.6%). Although the results did not indicate measurable schizophrenia incidence among the Hispanic sample, these subjects are likely to have other mental disorders, psychoses (59.4%) and affective psychoses (40%). In sum, Blacks who have mental disorders tend to have schizophrenia more often than Whites and Hispanics, but are less likely to develop manic depressive psychosis.

When mental disorders were analyzed according to age, schizophrenia emerged as a young adult's disease with 51% of people with schizophrenia it between the ages of 25 and 34. The category "other psychoses" was mainly seen in the older age groups. These results provide evidence that a relationship exists between age and type of mental disorder.

Among the employed, the most prevalent mental disorder was schizophrenia (59.2%), followed by affective psychoses (22.3%) and other psychoses (18.5%). For the group "not in the labor force", the order of prevalence was schizophrenia (39%), other psychoses (37.4%) and affective psychoses (23.6%). An interesting observation was that among the unemployed, the entire sample (100%) suffered from affective psychoses.

Finally, on the basis of income, findings showed very little (1.9%) evidence of mental disorders among persons who earned $50,000 or more. In contrast, findings show more than one-third (35.6%) of the mental disorders group were at the opposite end of the income scale. More specifically, persons earning between $7,000 and $9,999 per year represented 37.6% of the schizophrenia sample, 35.4% of the affective psychoses sample and 33.5% of the other psychoses sample. These findings suggest a high negative correlation between the prevalence of certain mental disorders and level of income. In other words, as income increases, selected mental disorders decrease.

Nervous Conditions

For the total group of nervous conditions, the three most prevalent were mental retardation (37.1%), cerebral palsy (28.3%) and epilepsy (19.2%). The findings indicate that when examined by race, nervous conditions were found to be more prevalent among Whites. Of the total population reporting these conditions, 78.1% were White, 15.4% were Black, 5% were Hispanic and 1.4% were other. The trend for associating the highest rates of nervous conditions according to race appear to be mental retardation (Black), cerebral palsy (Black), Parkinson Disease (other), epilepsy (other), multiple sclerosis (White),and other disorders (White).

When examined by age, mental retardation was most prevalent among persons between six and 16 years of age. These results also show that the incidence of Parkinson Disease increases as a person ages with onset of the disease emerging between ages 35 and 44 (1.9%) and steadily increasing up to the over 74 age group (43.4%).

The data indicate that of the six nervous conditions under study, mental retardation and epilepsy account for more than 90% of all nervous conditions reported for subjects aged 16 years and under. While the 1986 sample of young people under age six were affected more frequently by mental retardation (52.3%) than by epilepsy (31.4%), a dramatic shift was seen for 1987. Within the 1987 cohort of children under age six, a sharp increase was seen in epilepsy (50.1%) and also a modest decrease in mental retardation (43.6%). According to these statistics, the incidence of epilepsy as a nervous condition appears to be rising rather quickly among children. This information raises question concerning reasons for lower reported incidence of mental retardation. Speculation includes the possibility that greater care is now being taken to correctly classify clients. Consequently, fewer persons may be labeled mentally retarded.

The 1986 and 1987 statistics also suggest that for selected groups between ages 25 and 64, there seemed to be trend lines toward or away from certain nervous conditions. For example, within certain age groups, multiple sclerosis percentage rates decreased from 1986 to 1987. For the 45-54 age group, however, a moderate increase was shown. Increases for "other disorders" were reported from the 45-54 (10.1%) and 55-64 (7%) age groups, while a moderate decline (9.3%) was seen in the 25-34 age group. Cerebral palsy appeared stable over the two-year time block. A comparison of disability across age categories shows a trend for prevalence of nervous conditions to be closely associated with age. Nervous conditions which are frequent in selected age groups are virtually nonexistent for others.

Finally, on the basis of income, 1986 findings show the most prevalent nervous conditions for persons earning between $5,000 and $6,999 were mental retardation (57.1%), cerebral palsy (17.8%) and epilepsy (17.1%). For 1987 earnings between $5,000 and $6,000 the prevalence was cerebral palsy (37.6%), mental retardation (33.6%) and epilepsy (16.9%). The fact that a dramatic decrease (23.5%) was seen in mental retardation and a sharp increase (19.8%) was seen in cerebral palsy shows that the two conditions exchanged ranks in prevalence. The most prevalent nervous conditions for persons earning between $7,000 and $9,999 per year were mental retardation (35%), cerebral palsy (31.2%) and epilepsy (24.6%). The most prevalent nervous conditions in the $35,000 - $34,999 income range were mental retardation (41.1%), cerebral palsy (27.9%) and epilepsy (19.2%). This pattern was altered slightly for the $50,000 and above income group with the latest results showing mental retardation (31.3%), epilepsy (24.5%), and cerebral palsy (19.8%) highest in prevalence.

IMPACT OF IMPAIRMENTS

It is important to mention here that the conditions examined in this study have a significant impact on the lives of individuals with disabilities. The prevalence and incidence of these conditions, particularly various physical impairments, seem to greatly influence the extent to which an individual can work, and the amount of income they earn.

Effect on Income at Various Ages

In 1982, disabled workers who came on the social security disability insurance rolls from mid-1980 to mid-1981 had median monthly incomes of less than $500 if they were unmarried and less than $1,300 if they were married. These median monthly income levels, which included the income of a spouse and minor children if present, were roughly half those of the general population of people aged 35-64. Social security benefits were the most important source of income for workers with disabilities and their families. They accounted for 40 percent of the total income of unmarried workers with disabilities. Social security benefits provided at least half of all income for more than 80 percent of unmarried beneficiaries with disabilities and for 50 percent of the married beneficiaries.

For married beneficiaries with disabilities, earnings of the spouse were the second most important income source. Spousal earnings accounted for 28 percent of total income. Pensions and asset income each accounted for about 10 percent of total income for married beneficiaries.

Earnings were not an important source of income for unmarried beneficiaries since they amounted to only about three percent of total income. Pensions, asset income, and public transfers each accounted for about ten percent of total income of the unmarried beneficiaries.

In the present study, at the age 45-54 range, the impact of a disability on income was virtually the same for all six types of impairments. The income for this age group was approximately $21,000 per year. At age 55 and beyond, there was a dramatic lowering of income. This may be due to retirement from the work force. Not much confidence can be placed in the broad disparity seen for the 17-24 age range because it could be due to a number of factors, including teenage unemployment, and also the fact that persons in this age group have not yet benefited from rehabilitation.

Among Blacks between the ages of 25 and 44, the impairment with the most devastating impact on income was loss of extremity. Among persons with loss of an extremity the income was zero at both the 25-34 and 35-44 age ranges. After age 44, there was a steady increase in median income for this group until it reached $10,000 at age 65. It is conjectured that this increase may be due either to the assignment of benefits, or to successful rehabilitation, or some combination of the two.

The impact of speech disorder among Blacks was particularly perplexing. The median income for persons with a speech disorder was less than $3,000 at the age range of 17-24. At the range of 45-54, however, there was a sharp increase to about $21,000 per year. This shift was followed by a sharp decline at age 55-64, where income dropped to about $7,000 per year.

Among the hearing impaired, the median family income was relatively stable from age 25 through 64, hovering around the $8,000 to $10,000 range. There was a drop, however, at the 65-74 range to about $6,000, possibly due to this group leaving the work force. It may be worthy of special note that at the 17-24 age range, income was highest for persons with a hearing impairment

19

(about $17,000) and lowest for persons with a speech disorder (about $2,000).

The impact of physical impairment on Blacks was in sharp contrast to its impact on Whites. With the exception of paralysis where the median White family income was around $3,000 per year, the income for disabled Whites was significantly higher across the entire life span. Moreover, the variability in income associated with different types of impairments was considerably less. While median family income among Blacks hovered around $8,000, the income for Whites was closer to $18,000. With the exception of paralysis and speech disorder, the trend lines for all other impairments were virtually the same. It seems safe to conclude from this information that among Whites the impact of having a disability was much less severe than it was for Blacks, and that the effects of different kinds of disability are much less variable. In others words, being disabled and White is much less devastating than being disabled and Black.

The variation in impact observed for Blacks was even more pronounced for Hispanics, but the trend lines suggest that median income among most impaired groups was somewhat higher for Hispanics. An exception was noted for speech disorders, where the trend was very irregular and which also showed a median income of zero at age range 25-34, 35-44, 45-54 and 65-74. A zero median income was also seen for the loss of extremity group at ages 17-24 and 35-44. In spite of these departures, however, the median family income for Hispanics across all impairment groups and ages, was slightly higher than it was for Blacks.

Impact of Impairment on Ability to Work at Various Ages

Among persons reporting that they were not limited in their ability to work, the speech disorder and paralysis groups reported the lowest incomes at the youngest age range (17-24). The median income at this range was close to zero. Interestingly, it was also close to zero for the speech disorder group at the 25-34 age range. The median income for this group was also considerably lower than for other impairment groups at the 35-44 and the 55-64 age ranges. This information suggests that having a speech disorder affects one's income in ways that go beyond the person's ability to work. The specific nature of this influence should be a matter of considerable importance to persons working in this field.

20

In this report there is evidence suggesting that there may be more than one set of generic causes of speech disorder and that they relate to ability to work in different ways. Across all impairments and age groups the median family income tended to hover around $20,000 per year, except as noted above, for impaired persons reporting no limitation in their ability to work.

Among persons reporting that they were unable to work the greatest impact was seen for the impairment group with loss of extremities at the age range of 25-34. The income for this group was reported as zero. However, there was a sharp increase for this group to about $19,000 per year at age 35-44. This was followed by a drop to $10,000 at age 45-54, where it remained stable through age 74.

Between the ages of 25 and 64 there was similarly in the influence of paralysis, visual impairment and hearing loss among persons who were unable to work. The median income at the various age intervals paralleled each other for these groups. Essentially, this same type of pattern was seen for persons reporting a limitation in the kind or amount of work they could do.

DISCUSSION

It is of importance to our understanding of disability to note that females experience more chronic debilitating health conditions, but males experience more physical impairments. Males appear to be more susceptible to certain types of disabling conditions such as loss of extremities, speech disorders, and paralysis.

Moreover, findings from this study suggest that disability as a result of physical impairments appears to have a more pernicious effect than disability as a consequence of chronic health conditions. A case in point is that there is a pronounced tendency for persons at higher education levels to be less affected by chronic health conditions. With regard to employment, over half of all adults with a chronic conditions earn less than $20,000 per year, while the impairments with the most deleterious impact for Black males (speech and paralysis of the extremities) in particular, was observed in the income range between $0 - $10,000 per year. These facts alone serve to underscore the significance of defining what we mean when we use the term "disability." Prevalence reports based on some vague and amorphous term such as "the disabled" are likely to be very misleading, if not outright erroneous. The danger in this practice is that decisions may be made and policies formulated which will not be based on an accurate perception of the problem.

When examined according to race and ethnicity, the most prevalent chronic health conditions were as follows: Whites - arthritis; Blacks - high blood pressure; Hispanics - high blood pressure. Hispanics for the most part, were proportionately underrepresented in all chronic conditions with the exception of diabetes which was found to exist in excess of the Hispanic representation in the population. Blacks, however, were proportionately overrepresented for the specific chronic conditions of cerebrovascular disease, diabetes, and high blood pressure.

When examined on the basis of age, the two most prevalent chronic health conditions across all three working age groups (17-24, 25-44, 45-64) were invertebral disc disorders and high blood pressure. There is a dramatic increase in the prevalence of chronic health conditions as one ages, but this increase is sharpest for arthritis, cerebrovascular disease, diabetes, and heart disease. Over three-fourths of all persons suffering from a chronic health problem were over the age of 44.

For impairments, the highest rates according to race were hearing - White, orthopedic - Hispanics, visual - White, paralysis - Blacks, loss of extremities -Blacks, and speech disorder - Blacks. Among Hispanics, the highest impairment rates were seen for orthopedic and absence of extremities. Impairments involving considerable incapacity, such as paralysis or loss of extremities, are much more likely to occur among Blacks than among other ethnic groups. The results of this study show that approximately one in six persons with paralysis of the extremities is Black. Paralysis of the extremities has profound implications for one's ability to work, since many employment opportunities require ability to use the upper and lower limbs to some degree.

When these impairments were further examined on the basis of employment status, it was found that the highest rate of unemployed (including persons who considered themselves not in the labor force) was observed for paralysis of extremities, absence of extremities and speech disorders. Among the six impairment groups, these conditions exact their heaviest toll on Blacks. Thus, it appears that minorities, especially Blacks, are more prone to suffer a deleterious impact on employment and subsequent income based on the type of disability they are more likely to have. Additional findings show that impaired persons who are employed have a family income which is approximately $10,000 higher than that of impaired persons who are not in the labor force.

Some of the mystery surrounding the impact of speech disorder on median income is removed when we more closely observe the relationship between impairment and age. Over 40% of persons with a speech disorder are below the age of 17. This helps to explain the low median income for the speech disorder group, since a large number are not in the labor force. After dropping in the middle age ranges (35-44; 45-54) the prevalence of speech disorder rises again in old age. This may be due to the fact that speech disorder has a very different etiology in old age as compared to childhood. In old age it is likely to be related to some other physical impairment such as stroke, or a nervous system disorder, while in young children it is likely to be related to stuttering, stammering, articulation or muteness. Moreover, there is steady increase in the percentage of persons afflicted with hearing and visual disorders as we proceed upward in age across the life span.

The overwhelming majority of impaired persons were either married and living with a spouse, widowed, or had never married. Interesting, one of out of every three impaired persons lives in the southern part of the country. Of the four geographic areas, the South has the highest prevalence rates for all six impairments under study. Speech disorders, visual impairments, and absence of extremities were especially prominent in this region.

Of particular concern is the impact of limitations of activity on one's ability to work and to perform daily activities. Over one third of persons experiencing some type of impairment reported no limitation in work or general activity. On the other hand, approximately 14.7% were limited, but not in their major functional activity. Nine percent were limited in work activity. Constraints were observed, however, for the paralysis group where over 70% reported a limitation or an inability to engage in major functional or work activity. Among persons with limitations of activity resulting from either impairments or chronic health conditions, Blacks are overrepresented in proportion to their numbers in the general population.

The income level for people with disabilities Is substantially lower than that of non-disabled persons. The average household income for the general population in 1988 was $34,017 per year. In contrast, the median family income for people with disabilities was around $18,000. A comparison of the two income levels shows that the income levels of persons in the general populations exceed that of persons with disabilities by as much as 47%. When examined according to race, it is evident

23

that White persons with disabilities are generally in the low income range ($18,000), but not as destitute as Hispanics ($12,000) or Blacks ($8,000), whose family income levels fall below the poverty index reported in the latest census ($12,091). The situation is especially acute for Blacks with disabilities when income lag behind those of Whites with disabilities by at least $10,000 per year. In addition, people in the general population have income levels which more than quadruple those of Black people with disabilities. Overall, it appears that income levels for Black people with disabilities are markedly lower than those of persons who are not disabled, Whites with disabilities and Hispanics with disabilities. By the same token, white persons with disabilities are also far below income levels of the non-disabled population.

In sum, these findings are essential to our understanding of disabilities and the impact that the prevalence of these disabilities has on ethnic minorities. In order to gain greater insights from these findings, more research is needed with respect to the etiology of these disabling conditions within ethnic groups.

References

Bowe, F. (1985a). African-American adults with disabilities. A statistical report drawn from Census Bureau data.

Bowe, F. (1985b). Disabled adults of Hispanic American origin. A statistical report drawn from Census Bureau data.

Thornhill, H.L., and HoSang, D.A. (1988). Poverty, race, and disability. In S. Walker, J.E. Fowler, R.W. Nicholls, and K. Turner (Eds.), Building bridges to independence: Employment, successes, problems, and needs of African-Americans with disabilities (pp. 148-156). Washington, DC: The Center for the Study of Handicapped Children and Youth, School of Education, Howard University.

Walker, S., Akpati, E., Roberts, V., Palmer, R., and Newsome, M. (1986). Frequency and distribution of disabilities among Blacks: Preliminary findings. In S. Walker, F.Z. Belgrave, A. Banner, and R.W. Nicholls (Eds.), Equal to the challenge: Perspectives, problems, and strategies in the rehabilitation of the nonwhite disabled (pp. 51-54). Washington, DC: Bureau of Educational Research, School of Education, Howard University.

Walker, S. (1987). Howard university research and training center for access to rehabilitation and economic opportunity (Project Award No. H133B80059-89). Washington, DC: National Institute on Disability and Rehabilitation Research, U.S. Department of Education.

DIFFERENCES IN REHABILITATION SERVICE UTILIZATION PATTERNS OF AFRICAN AMERICANS AND WHITE AMERICANS WITH DISABILITIES

FAYE Z. BELGRAVE, GEORGE WASHINGTON UNIVERSITY
SYLVIA WALKER, HOWARD UNIVERSITY

Abstract

The purpose of this study was to investigate differences in rehabilitation service utilization of African Americans and White Americans with disabilities. The results are based upon data collected from 228 clients at private and public rehabilitation facilities throughout the United States. The subjects were asked if they were receiving the following rehabilitation services: (1) physical therapy, (2) occupational therapy, (3) vocational rehabilitation, (4) social services, (5) other counseling services, and (6) follow-up care by a physician. Sample characteristics of the subjects (Mean age, age range, gender, marital status, education level, employment) are provided. The results of the study show that there are several differences in service utilization patterns of African Americans and White Americans with African Americans being at a disadvantage. Some reasons for these differences may be economic factors, access factors, attitudinal factors and referral problems.

Health care utilization patterns differ for African Americans and White Americans (U.S. Department of Health and Human Services, 1990). For example, African Americans (compared to Whites) are less likely to visit their physician at least once during a year and more likely to go longer periods of time between office visits. When African Americans are hospitalized they tend to have a longer length of stay which suggest that they are "sicker" when admitted to the hospital. While there have been a number of reports generated on health care utilizations patterns of African Americans and Whites, we have seen limited information on utilization patterns of African Americans with disabilities. The purpose of this study was to investigate differences in rehabilitation service utilization of African Americans and Whites with disabilities.

This research was sponsored by the National Institute of Disability and Rehabilitation Research.

METHOD

<u>Subjects and Data Collection</u>

This study was part of a larger study on psychosocial aspects of disabilities in ethnic minorities. Data were collected from 228 clients at private and public rehabilitation facilities in the Eastern, Western, and Mid-Western regions of the United States. Data were collected in 1985. Only data relevant to rehabilitation service utilization will be presented in this paper.

Subjects were randomly selected from the client rosters maintained at agencies and facilities participating in the study. The sample consisted of 170 African Americans and 45 White Americans with disabilities. Subjects who were not African American or White were not included in the analyses.

<u>Measure of Rehabilitation Service Utilization</u>

Subjects were asked to indicate whether or not they were receiving the following types of rehabilitation services: (1) physical therapy, (2) occupational therapy, (3) vocational rehabilitation, (4) social services, (5) other counseling services, and (6) follow-up care by physician.

RESULTS

<u>Description of Sample</u>

Sample characteristics are shown in Table 1. The two groups did not differ appreciatively on most of the demographic variables. The African American sample was comprised of more males (52.7%) and the White sample was comprised of more females (57.8%). White Americans also had a slightly higher level of education - 65.9% of Whites had an education at the high school level or higher versus 55.2% for African Americans. Finally, a higher percent of Whites than African Americans had higher levels of income from employment, 26.7% of Whites had income over $20,000 (versus only 8% of African Americans).

Medicaid was the largest source of medical insurance for both African Americans (52.9%) and Whites (57.5%). However, a larger percentage of Whites than African Americans reported having private insurance, 35% in contrast to 25.8%.

TABLE 1

Sample Characteristics

	African Americans	**White Americans**
Mean Age	44.5	43.2
Age Range	21-82	21-83
Gender	47.3% Female 52.7% Male	57.8% Female 42.2% Male
Marital status	24.4% Married 64.9% Single 10.7% Widowed	22.2% Married 75.6% Single 2.2% Widowed
Education level	44.8% < H.S. 55.2% > H.S.	34.1% < H.S. 65.9% < H.S.
Employment Status	20.2% Employed 78.8% Not Employed	22.2% Employed 77.8% Not Employed
Income from Employment	55.0% < $5,000 7.0% $5,000-10,000 20.0% $10,000-20,000 8.0% > $20,000	50.0% < $5,000 10.0% $5,000-10,000 13.3% $10,000-20,000 26.7% > $20,000

Differences in Rehabilitation Service Utilization Patterns Between African Americans and Whites

Chi-squares analyses were computed with race (Black or White) and rehabilitation service use (yes or no) as variables. The significance level was set at .05.

African Americans were less likely than Whites to report that they were receiving physical therapy (p. < .001). Twenty percent of the African Americans reported receiving physical therapy and 41% of Whites reported receiving physical therapy.

Only three percent of African Americans reported receiving occupational therapy while 34% of White Americans reported receiving occupational therapy (p < .0001).

Twenty percent of African Americans reported receiving counseling services while 46% of White Americans reported receiving counseling services - a difference significant at the .001 level.

African Americans were less likely to report receiving social services (49% compared to 55% for White Americans). However, this difference was not statistically significant.

There was no significant difference between the percentage of African Americans and Whites who reported receiving vocational rehabilitation services. Approximately 31.2% of African Americans and 29.5% of Whites reported receiving vocational rehabilitation.

Contrary to expectations, there was no significant difference in the frequencies with which African Americans and White Americans reported seeing medical personnel. Twenty-nine percent of African Americans and 27.3% of Whites reported receiving follow-up care by a physician.

African Americans were much more likely to report that their primary source of transportation to medical appointments was public transportation, 34% for African Americans compared to 7% for Whites (p < .005).

Perception of Interference of Disability

It was also of interest to determine if there was a difference in whether African Americans and Whites perceived their disability as interfering in activities of daily living. T-test were done to test for mean differences in perceptions between the two groups. While reporting fewer rehabilitation services, African Americans (compared to Whites) were more likely to perceive their disability as interfering in daily activities such as employment (p < .05) and physical activities (p < .01).

DISCUSSION

Before discussing the implications of the findings, it is necessary to emphasize that the study findings should be interpreted cautiously. The sample is not a national random sample. Therefore, participants are not representative of all persons with disabilities. Furthermore, all participants in this study were affiliated in some way with a rehabilitation agency or facility since this was a requirement for study participation. Therefore, this study sample may be different from the larger sample of persons with disabilities who may not be affiliated with a rehabilitation clinic or agency.

The results of this study indicate that there are several differences in rehabilitation service utilization patterns of African Americans and Whites with African Americans being at a disadvantage. A variety of explanations may be provided for these differences. They are summarized below.

1.   **Economic Factors.** African Americans were not as represented in the higher income group, therefore, finances may in part, account for differences in services. African Americans were also less likely to have private insurance coverage than Whites. Private insurance coverage may cover the cost of some rehabilitation services.

2.   **Access Factors.** It may be more difficult for African Americans than Whites to go for rehabilitation services and medical appointments. A higher percentage of African Americans reported that they used public transportation to go to medical appointments. Furthermore, clinics, hospitals, and other medical facilities may be further away from predominately African Americans neighborhoods where African Americans may live.

3.   **Attitudinal factors.** Beliefs in the efficacy of rehabilitation services may differ for African Americans and Whites. African Americans may hold beliefs that rehabilitation services such as physical therapy and occupational therapy may not benefit them far as their disability status is 'God's will.' More research is needed to clarify how beliefs and attitudes may impact rehabilitation service utilization.

4.   **Referrals to Rehabilitation Services.** We did not address the question of whether or not rehabilitation referrals for certain services differed for African Americans and Whites, but this could account for differences. Interestingly, the same percentage of African Americans and Whites reported receiving vocational rehabilitation services.

The findings from this study suggest the need for further work in this area. Before planning programs to increase rehabilitation service utilization of African Americans, we need a clearer understanding of why these differences exist.

Reference

U.S. Department of Health and Human Services (1990). Health Status of the Disadvantaged. Department of Health and Human Services, Publication No. (HRSA) HRS-P-DV90-1, Washington, DC.

SUBSTANCE ABUSE AMONG PHYSICALLY DISABLED PATIENTS IN A HOSPITAL SERVING URBAN MINORITIES

HERBERT L. THORNHILL, DENNIS HOSANG,
THOMAS B. HART, AND MARIA RIVERA
DEPARTMENT OF REHABILITATION MEDICINE
COLUMBIA UNIVERSITY, HARLEM HOSPITAL CENTER
NEW YORK CITY

Abstract

This article provides preliminary data for a four year study of substance abuse and physical disability including the prevalence of substance abuse among people with disabilities is currently underway at Harlem Hospital Center in New York. Subjects consist of hospital patients referred to the Department of Rehabilitation Medicine with diagnoses that include both physical impairment(s) and substance abuse. Data are being collected through structured interviews by health care providers and from medical records. This report includes preliminary data on the first 38 subjects, mean age 49, 25 males and 13 females. The majority reported use of more than one substance. The most frequently reported drug was alcohol, either solely or in combination with others, cocaine, heroin, crack, and marijuana use was also common. The three most frequently reported impairments found among IVDU's were: generalized deconditioning associated with acute illnesses, skin ulcers, and fractures due to various forms of trauma. Half of the IVDU's were HIV positive. These preliminary findings support the concern that there exists a large unmet need for treatment and prevention as regards substance abuse and people with disabilities.

INTRODUCTION

There is considerable discussion among experts concerning trends of the national substance abuse epidemic. A prevailing view (New York Times, 1990) holds that there is a diverging pattern of drug use in the United States according to socioeconomic class: better educated middle class people report less drug use, while less educated people from the poorest communities continue to use drugs, and in some cases at an increasing level. This would seem to explain the curious announcements from our highest government officials declaring great success in the so-called war on drugs, while we continue to witness mounting devastation by the effects in our setting. A clear danger to be avoided, is that as drugs become less a middle and upper class problem, policymakers may place this issue on the back burner of the national agenda. Poor and minority communities would again be left to deal with the problem with little outside help. In New York City, general trends show little change in the epidemic.

Similarly, as concerns disability, there is a prevalence gap, with no evidence of narrowing, between the poor and non-white populations as compared with the general population. Census data indicate 14.1% of the African American working age population is disabled as compared to 8.4% for Whites (U.S. Census, 1989). High rates of disease and trauma in poor and minority communities correlate strongly with their high rates of disabling conditions. The McCord and Freeman study (1990) of Harlem Hospital highlights this reality. They reported a mortality rate for African Americans in Harlem more than double that of White Americans in the United States and a survival rate for African American men less than that for men in Bangladesh, considered one of the poorest countries in the world.

A review of the literature on substance abuse and physical disability reveals increasing, though still insufficient, interest among health care providers, government agencies, and consumers. Accounts in trade publications reflect service provider and payee concerns with containment and general management of the problem. Scientific articles describe drug effects on various body systems, including relationships with the HIV epidemic.

Jeffrey Kreutzer (1989) of the Medical College of Virginia, studied drug and alcohol use, pre- and post - injury among a group of traumatically brain injured persons. He reported that half the sample had high blood levels at the time of injury and that 10% to 20% continued to abuse alcohol after injury. Curtis et. al. (1986) surveyed 200 medicine and surgery patients at Harlem Hospital Center and found an alcoholism prevalence rate of 30.2% among medical patients and an association with progressively serious depression and dementia. Prevalence among surgery patients was 18.3%. Thornhill and co-workers (1986) also of Harlem Hospital, studied major lower extremity amputations associated with parenteral drug use. Among this group, injections of "speedballs" (mixtures of cocaine and heroin) into the femoral vessels led to pseudoaneurysms associated with 15 amputations. Despite good motor potential and relative youth, the overall group of 64 persons with 72 amputations had a low rate of successful use of protheses.

Another and perhaps more ominous expression of this co-morbid syndrome is the increasing number of problem infants with developmental disabilities born to substance abusing mothers. The Department of Health and Human Services (New York Times, 1990) released a study that reported nearly 9000 babies born in 1989 to mothers addicted to crack. The writer estimated that there could be as many as four million such infants in this country by the year 2000. These babies are often born neurologically impaired. Many have additional physical, emotional, and social deficits which compound their disability. We do not know the complete and long-term outcome of children of substance abusers. Sharry Daren (1986) of the New York State Division of Substance Abuse Services (DSAS) studied children of substance abusers (COSA) in the New York City methadone treatment system. She found that the effects of drugs on neonates include: low birth weight, irritability, excessive crying, and eating and sleeping disorders during the first year of life. By the end of the first year, many showed developmental problems such as poor motor control, visual problems, and poor attention.

It is believed that substance abuse is not only a contributor, through disease and trauma, to a variety of disabling conditions, but also continues to be a problem after disablement for timely recovery and full independence. Rehabilitation professionals and service providers are expressing concern about the impact of drug and alcohol use on the rehabilitation process and its outcomes. The concern is often expressed in professional journals (Wade, 1990) and is evidenced by a number of local conferences and seminars for professionals on the management of alcohol and drug abuse in the treatment setting. Others (Pelizzoni, 1989) have observed that many clinicians ignore the substance abuse problems of their patients and they are generally not oriented or prepared to help patients with disabilities with this problem. The impetus for dealing with the problem is likely to come from rehabilitation managers and payee of services. Addiction can prolong treatment and inflate cost. Case managers for insurance companies often report cases that medically could be resolved in months but took years because of drug and alcohol use.

The purpose of this four year study (1990-1993) is to expand the body of knowledge concerning various aspects of the rehabilitation process as it relates to substance abuse. Research findings will provide a foundation for the expansion of rehabilitation services as they relate to restorative care for a largely minority, medically indigent group of persons with physical disabilities.

The Department of Rehabilitation Medicine at Harlem Hospital Center, under the sponsorship of the Howard University Research and Training Center, has undertaken a study of the relationship of substance abuse and physical disability among persons referred to this facility for restorative care. The study sample consists of hospital patients whose diagnoses include these two (2) entities.

This paper represents a preliminary report including the presentation of some initial data. We emphasize that these are only preliminary data gathered during the first six months of the study.

METHODOLOGY

Subjects

The initial sample consists of 38 subjects. Subjects are hospital patients referred for rehabilitation services and by virtue of referral have a potentially disabling physical impairment. These consultation requests are screened for substance abuse, defined as either alcohol and/or illegal drug abuse. Diagnoses are reported by the consulting physician and confirmed by a second departmental physician.

A brief description of the setting can be useful. Harlem is located in Northern Manhattan, New York City. It is one of the most homogeneous communities in the city with 96% African Americans, most of whom have migratory roots in the Southeastern United States. Harlem was the fulcrum of the African American culture renaissance in the 1920's and continues today to be a center for African American identity and culture. Its cultural preeminence belies its social, economic, and health crisis. Reference has already been made to a report of excess mortality more than twice U.S. Whites and more than rates found in Bangladesh. The tuberculosis rate is one of the highest in the western hemisphere. Median family income is 30% of the national level, and only 50% of all other African Americans in the country. Only 51% of males between the ages 21 and 26 are employed. Harlem Hospital is the major provider of health care services to the population, and the Department of Rehabilitation Medicine is the primary provider of acute rehabilitation services.

Data Collection

Identified subjects are interviewed by a physician during their hospital stay, using a structured questionnaire. Supplemental data are obtained through review of subjects' medical charts. The data base includes demographics, medical history and diagnoses, detailed substance abuse and treatment history, attitude towards substance abuse, and an offer or a referral for treatment of the substance abuse problem.

RESULTS

From August 1, 1989 through February 28, 1990, 92 patients were referred to the Department of Rehabilitation Medicine with dual diagnoses of physical impairment(s) and substance abuse. That number represents 8.2% of all patients in-patients referred to the Service during this period. Of these 92 cases, 64 were interviewed and 38 cases were included in the study sample. There were twice as many males as females. African Americans constituted 90% of the sample, reflecting the local community; the remainder of the sample were Hispanics. The mean age, 49 years, is younger than the mean age, 56 years, for the total population refered to this Department.

In terms of drug use, prior to hospitalization, the most frequently reported drug was alcohol, 83% reporting such use. Slightly over half of the sample used either cocaine (58%), or heroin (56%). One-third of the sample used crack and/or marijuana. The majority of the sample were polydrug users, characterized by a pattern of abuse which included use of intravenous drugs, crack, marijuana, and alcohol. Alcohol was the only drug reported used not in combination with others.

Injected drug use was reported by about two-thirds of the sample. People who were intravenous drug users (IVDUs) tended to be multiple drug abusers. The approximately one-third who did not inject were primarily alcohol abusers and tended not to abuse substances other than alcohol. There were gender and age differences between non-IVDUs and IVDUs. The non-IVDU's, primarily alcoholics, were more evenly distributed between male and female and tended to be older than the IVDU group.

The three most frequent impairments found among this group of IVDUs were deconditioning associated with acute illnesses, skin ulcers, and fractures. Deconditioning in this sample was associated most commonly with infections secondary to Human Immuno-deficiency Virus (HIV). Skin ulcers were usually the result of chronic drug injection. Fractures among IVDUs were attributed to various forms of trauma.

We were also interested in determining whether patients themselves saw a connection between their hospitalization and substance history. IVDUs were much more likely, in comparison with alcoholics, to report such a connection: 75% of IVDUs versus 50% of alcoholics reported a connection between the drug abuse and current hospitalization. For the entire sample, 63% said they saw a connection, while the physician saw a connection between the drug abuse and hospitalization in 60.6%.

In addition to IVDUs greater awareness of the connection between hospitalization and their substance abuse, IVDUs compared to alcoholics were also more likely to have received treatment for their drug abuse. Seventy percent of IVDUs compared to 17% of alcoholics had received treatment at sometime.

Half of the IVDUs were HIV positive. This is consistent with IVDUs infectivity rate reported by others. The direct relationship between injected drug use and the acuteness of medical complications associated with the HIV disorders may make the drug use-hospital connection more salient for IVDUs than alcoholics.

IVDUs were twice as likely to report having family or friends who used drugs than were alcoholics. Alcoholics were overwhelmingly less likely to want assistance for their drug problem, with only 9% expressing this need. However, almost half of the IVDUs requested this assistance. The need to involve family and friends in the recovery process and the need to be more aggressive in an intervention approach is suggested. Poor prognosis for abstinence is indicated.

CONCLUSION

The data presented in this study must be regarded with caution because of the small number of subjects and incomplete analysis. These preliminary findings begin to offer some insight into the problems of dual diagnoses of physical disability and substance abuse in this community. The data suggests that presenting impairments and causes may relate to predominant mode and type of substance abused. The greater social acceptability of alcoholism than injected drug use may account in large for the less likelihood of alcoholics to have been treated for their abuse, to desire treatment for their abuse, or see a connection between their substance abuse and their hospitalization.

The medical diagnostic characteristics of this sample suggest that the initiation of drug abuse, at an early age resulted in repeated onslaughts to the body over a number of years from drugs, trauma, disease, hospitalization, and progressively worsening impairments and disabilities. This has resulted in the quality of lives being severely compromised. The downward spiral of health problems and impairments has made intervention for alcohol and drug use particularly difficult. Now the phenomenon of crack use poses an even greater challenge.

References

Curtis, J. et. al. (1986). Prevalence rates of alcoholism, associated depression and dementia on Harlem Hospital medicine and surgical services. Advances in Alcohol and Substance Abuse, 6, 45-65.

Daren, S. (1986). Children of substance abuse. Journal of Substance Abuse Treatment, 3, 77-79.

Kreutzer, J.S., Leininger, B.E., Sherron, P., and Groah, C. (1989). Management of psychosocial dysfunction following traumatic brain injury to improve employment outcome. In P. Wehman and J. Kreutzer (Eds.). Vocational rehabilitation after traumatic brain injury. Rockville, MD: Aspen Publishers, Inc.

McCord, C. and Freeman, H.P. (1990). Excess mortality in Harlem. New England Journal of Medicine, 322, 173-177.

Pelizzoni, V. (May, 1989) Double Trouble. New Jersey Rehabilitation, 20-24.

Rich vs. poor: Drug patterns are diverging. New York Times, (1987, August 30).

Study of addicted babies hints vast costs. New York Times, (1990, March 17).

Thornhill, H.L. and HoSang, D.A. (1988). Poverty, race and disability. In S. Walker, J.W. Fowler, R.W. Nicholls, & K.A. Turner (eds.) Building bridges to independence: Employment, success, problems and needs of African Americans with disabilities, 148-156. Washington, DC: The Center for the Study of Handicapped Children and Youth, School of Education, Howard University.

Thornhill, H.L. and Torres, L. (1986) Some observations on African Americans and physical disabilities. In S. Walker, Belgrave, F.Z., Banner, A.M., & Nichools, R.W. (Eds.). Equal to the challenge: Perspectives, problems and strategies in the rehabilitation of non-white disabled, 51-54. Washington, DC: Bureau of Education Research, Howard University

U.S. Department of Commerce. (1989). Labor force status and other characteristics of persons with a work disability: 1981-1988. Superintendent of Documents, U.S. Government Printing Office, Washington, DC.

Wade, J. (February/March, 1990). Can't just say no. Rehab Management. 60-66.

SECTION 11

FUTURE FRONTIERS

NEW FRONTIERS IN MULTICULTURAL APPROACHES

ENHANCING DIVERSITY: A MULTICULTURAL EMPLOYMENT PERSPECTIVE

LYNDA R. CAMPBELL
DEPARTMENT OF COMMUNICATION DISORDERS
SAINT LOUIS UNIVERSITY

Abstract

Minority individuals are more likely to have a work disability than non-minorities. Nevertheless, these same individuals disproportionately suffer from unemployment as well as under-employment. Therefore, it is important to critically examine the work setting in order to create an environment that is multicultural and conducive for all employees. There are a number of barriers including educational attainment, lack of skills, lack of understanding of the world of work culture, miscommunication due to other cultural differences and stereotypes, fear, prejudice, and discrimination. Strategies for the maintenance of employment are conducting a multicultural employment self-analysis, hiring a cultural broker, and providing cross-cultural training.

Much has been written about projected demographic shifts within the United States. Demographic projections of the next several decades reveal that today's minority groups within the United States will comprise approximately one-third of its total population (U.S. Bureau of the Census, 1983). It is estimated that by the turn of the century, today's minorities will also consist of one-third of the net additions to the labor force. It is projected that 21.8 million such persons will be in the labor force (Johnston et al., 1987). Included in this labor force will be minority persons with disabilities.

Although such demographic figures lend credibility to the increasing cultural and ethnic diversity within the United States, they also confront us with a formidable challenge. These same individuals disproportionately suffer from unemployment, as well as under-employment, inadequate education, poor health, and other economic and social barriers (American Council on Education and the Education Commission of the States, 1988; President's Committee on Employment of the Handicapped, 1986; Thorne, 1988). However, the nation must provide full equality and participation for all of its citizens, including minorities as well as those with disabilities if it is going to continue to prosper as a world leader. The extent to which minorities with disabilities participate in and contribute to the economy will influence the continuing strength of the nation. This article will discuss changing demographics in the United States relative to present employment trends for minority individuals with disabilities. Several variables which may impede continued employment of minority persons with disabilities as well as strategies for the maintenance of employment are also discussed.

CHANGING DEMOGRAPHICS AND EMPLOYMENT

As the growth rates for minorities increase, the number of such individuals who can contribute and are needed to participate in the workforce will also increase. Presumably, as the growth rates of populations increase, the number of such individuals with disabilities will also increase. However, it is also assumed that advances in technology, increased access to services, treatment of curable diseases, as well as other factors will occur as the demographics change and will, therefore, result in a smaller proportion of minority individuals with disabilities in the future compared to the present.

Such demographic changes are significant given the changing labor market in the United States and the realization that the nation will have to rely on able-bodied minorities as well as minority persons with disabilities in order to meet employment demands of the 21st century (Walker, 1988). A disability refers to a health condition that prevents a person from working and/or restricts the amount or kind of work that a person can do (President's Committee on Employment of the Handicapped, 1985). Reportedly, there are approximately 13 million persons between the ages of 16 and 64 years who are classified as having a work disability. Of this figure, over 3 million have annual earnings below the poverty level (U.S. Bureau of the Census, 1983). Over half (57%) of all working-age disabled minority adults live with incomes below the official poverty level. The presence of a work disability is associated with a greater chance of being unemployed and with lower earnings.

Minority individuals are more likely to have a work disability than non-minorities. This may be due in part to the fact that minority individuals are more likely to perform physically demanding work which may lead to a disability. Additionally, medical conditions which may be corrected by non-minority individuals, may persist for minorities and result in permanent disabilities (President's Committee on Employment of the Handicapped, 1989).

Non-minority men with disabilities are employed twice as frequently as their minority peers. A typical working-age minority adult has less than a 10th grade education, is not in the labor force and has about $3,000 in income from all sources. A typical working-age non-minority adult has a high school education, is in the labor force and has about $7,500 in income from all sources. (President's Committee on Employment of the Handicapped, 1985).

BARRIERS IN THE EMPLOYMENT SETTING

A multicultural employment setting should identify and remove barriers which impede continued employment of minorities with disabilities. Such barriers to successful continued employment include: low educational attainment; not possessing the kinds of skills needed in the labor force; lack of knowledge of the world of work culture; individual cultural differences; stereotypes, prejudice, discrimination and racism; offensive language and; fear. Although the aforementioned variables may function as precursors to employment, they are also vital in the maintenance of employment. The above-mentioned variables do not afford persons within the employment setting the opportunity to experience the positive benefits of a diverse environment, thereby, not benefitting the employee, co-workers or employer. These barriers to continued successful employment are discussed briefly below.

Educational Attainment

Educational attainment has a strong effect on whether a person with a work disability is likely to be in the labor force. Minority adults with disabilities have lower levels of educational attainment than do non-minorities with disabilities, and non-disabled individuals (President's Committee on Employment of the Handicapped, 1985).

Participation in higher education is an important measure of well-being in our country. Institutions of higher education are relied upon to impart the knowledge and skills that will prepare individuals for employment roles which are crucial to the well-being of the nation. Educational non-advancement by a substantial portion of the citizens of the United States is a cause for deep concern, especially at a time of technological advances and global competition (American Council on Education and the Education Commission of the States, 1988). Currently, a disproportionate number of minority individuals with disabilities do not obtain a high school diploma or equivalency, resulting in low participation rates in higher education.

Most minorities with disabilities who are in the labor force are employed in minimum wage jobs which lack upward mobility. It is hypothesized that low levels of schooling may lead to participation in high-risk occupations. On the other hand, certain disabilities may make it more difficult to attend and complete school. Additionally, there may be a set of common factors (such as, economic deprivation in childhood) which may lead to low educational attainment and to an increased likelihood of becoming disabled (U.S. Bureau of the Census, 1983).

Skills In The Labor Force

An additional factor is the movement from an industrial to a technological society. Such a shift causes changes in the kinds of skills needed in the present as well as the future labor force. Individuals with disabilities are less likely to be employed in professional and technical occupations (U.S. Bureau of the Census, 1983). Although presently, minority individuals with disabilities are needed in professional and technical occupations, this need will become magnified as the growth rate of non-minorities lag behind minority growth rates. Nearly 25% of African-Americans with disabilities between the ages of 16-64 years do not have more than an 8th grade education. Such figures are also dismal for members of other minority groups (President's Committee on Employment of the Disabled, 1985). Therefore, special educators and rehabilitation professionals must examine, recommend and implement changes at the elementary and secondary levels so that the skills and potential of minority students with disabilities are maximized. Such a focus will improve the minority individual's opportunity to be competitive within the labor force. Such scrutiny will also increase the likelihood of minority individuals with disabilities acquiring the necessary skills and training through vocational rehabilitation and/or postsecondary education in order to be competitive in the labor force and a technological society.

The World of Work Culture

Cultural differences not only may contribute to difficulties in obtaining employment, but also in maintaining employment. Cultural differences include the "world of work" culture as well as the individual cultures of persons within the employment setting. The world of work cultures may be defined as whatever one needs to know or believe, in order to operate in a manner acceptable to individuals within the work setting. The world of work culture includes the rules of operation as well as determination of how one is to successfully manipulate and move within the employment setting. Many minority persons with disabilities may not understand the world of work culture. The reverse may also be true, the world of work culture may not be responsive to and/or incorporate the needs of minority individuals with disabilities.

Individual Cultural Differences

The cultures of persons within the work environment, including consumers, if appropriate, may be different from the culture of the minority individual with a disability. These differences may be due to differences as a result of a minority status as well as differences due to the cultures of able-bodied and individuals with disabilities. Differences among cultural groups in the United States are attributed to the histories and different world views, philosophies, and institutions unique to a particular culture. These cultural backgrounds are reflected in one's interactions and interpretations of the environment. The appropriateness or inappropriateness of behaviors depends on one's culture. However, it is important to also recognize that cultural values, ideas, and perceptions vary within a culture as well as across cultures (Collier, Ribeau and Hecht, 1986).

Stereotypes, Prejudice, Discrimination, and Racism

Individuals within the agency may possess stereotypes about disabilities which are compounded with stereotypes regarding minorities as a whole as well as particular minority groups. Such barriers may be further magnified by gender stereotypes. Factors that interfere with continued successful employment include outdated attitudes, negative self-image, and lack of positive role models depicting minority individuals with disabilities (Beck, 1988).

42

The attitudes of a society about minorities with disabilities are a reflection of the cumulative experiences of persons within that society (Walker, 1978; Walker, 1984). A historical examination of attitudes toward persons with disabilities across cultures suggests that attitudes toward disabilities have consistently relegated such persons to economic deprivation and dependency (Walker, 1988). Such negative attitudes regarding individuals with disabilities are compounded by an attitude of low expectation of minorities on the part of many non-minorities (Banner, 1988). The past solutions to these challenges have resulted in acts of charity, sympathy, rejection and condescension which contributed to the formation of a stereotype of unable, uneducable, unfit, and unacceptable in the employment sector (Thorne, 1988). Further, many non-minorities and able-bodied individuals may not be aware of stereotypes held due to their limited socialization with minority persons and persons with disabilities. Stereotypes may lead to prejudice, discrimination and racism. The minority disabled individual may experience prejudice and discrimination due to a disability which may be compounded with prejudice, discrimination and racism related to being a minority. Racism may include individual racism which may be held by other employees or co-workers as well as institutional racism (Banner, 1988).

Offensive Language

Individuals within the agency may utilize language that is offensive to a cultural or ethnic group being compounded with language that is offensive to persons with a disability. Many non-minority and able-bodied individuals may not be aware of language that is considered offensive due to limited contact with such persons. For example, use of words such as "victim" and "suffering with a disability" are offensive to many because they denote that the quality of life for persons with a disability is less meaningful than that of those without a disability.

Fear

The needs of certain persons with a disability may produce anxiety to some able-bodied employees and employers (e.g., how to handle seizures, injections, cardio-pulmonary resuscitation). Even being provided with specific instructions in case of an emergency may be alarming to some co-workers. Many able-bodied co-workers may have had limited contact with individuals with disabilities. Individuals within the employment setting may also experience an unconscious level of fear and lack of trust of minority individuals with disabilities based on underlying stereotypes, lack of knowledge and voluntary socialization with such persons. The presence of a person with a disability also makes persons aware of their own vulnerability hence, increasing tension and anxiety.

STRATEGIES FOR MAINTENANCE OF EMPLOYMENT

The challenges encountered by minority individuals with disabilities include the challenge of being a member of a racial minority group in America as well as the challenge of possessing a disability. Principles which may be applied to a multicultural employment setting which embraces disability as well as minority status may be derived from models which focus on the preparation of the individual as well as the preparation of the work environment.

Preparation of the Person with a Disability

Career preparation must be integrated into the entire educational curriculum of a person with a disability. To prepare minority individuals with disabilities for employment, their individual differences should be defined and understood, their strengths should be developed, their weaknesses should be counterbalanced, and their skills and interests should be matched to appropriate training and employment. Such career preparation will decrease unemployment as well as under-employment (Beck, 1988).

Preparation of the Employment Environment

Preparation of the employment environment may be performed in a number of ways. Of the numerous possibilities, three modified approaches will be discussed because of their strong potential for successful employment of minorities with disabilities. These approaches include: a multicultural employment self-analysis, use of a cultural broker, and the provision of cross-cultural training.

Approach #1 - A Multicultural Employment Self-Analysis

The work environment plays a vital role in the continued employment of minority persons with disabilities. Since such individuals obviously possess the requisite entrance skills for employment, it is important to examine the work setting in order to analyze an agency's commitment to developing a multicultural environment. Such efforts are important for the creation of an environment that is conducive for all employees. Below are a series of questions which can be utilized by an organization as part of its multicultural self-analysis.

Sample Questions to be Addressed in a Multicultural Employment Self-Analysis

1. Are there special recruitment efforts to hire minority individuals with disabilities?

2. Why are there special recruitment efforts to hire minority individuals with disabilities ?

3. Is recruitment a voluntary decision or one undertaken due to other factors?

4. What are the recruitment efforts for hiring minority persons with disabilities?

5. What are the minority recruitment goals and do these goals match the needs of the agency?

6. Are the recruitment procedures realistic relative to the recruitment goals and needs of the agency?

7. Who within the company is coordinating recruitment efforts?

8. Are there other individuals with disabilities employed within the agency? If so, what are the types of disabilities that members of the agency possess? In what positions are they employed?

9. Are there minority individuals with disabilities employed within the agency? If so, what are the types of disabilities these minority individuals posses? In what positions are they employed?

10. Has the work environment been "primed" for encompassing minority individuals with disabilities? If so, to what extent has the work environment been primed?

Many employment settings may have few, if any, able-bodied minority individuals, let alone such persons with disabilities. Hence, many work environments may not be reflective of the normal diversity found within the American society. In order to create a more diverse work environment, many employers may need to establish recruitment goals and procedures which include minorities

45

with disabilities. One may hypothesize that agencies with voluntary multicultural initiatives may possess a more positive environment than those created due to other factors. As previously mentioned, researchers have indicated that minority individuals with disabilities are more frequently employed in non-skilled positions with little likelihood of upward mobility as compared with disabled non-minorities or able-bodied minorities (President's Committee on Employment of the Handicapped, 1985; U.S. Bureau of the Census, 1983). Therefore, it is vital that employment settings embrace diversity. Such an embrace should include:

1.   An affirmation of diversity.

2.   Identification and removal of barriers to the maintenance of employment of minorities as well as barriers to individuals with disabilities.

3.   Effective employment recruitment strategies and goals for minority disabled individuals.

4.   A multicultural agency analysis.

5.   A belief that the potential of all can be maximized.

<u>Approach #2 - The Cultural Broker</u>

The cultural broker approach involves the utilization of supportive personnel placed on the job to function as a cultural broker in order to make the interaction between the persons of different cultures more effective. Gentemann and Whitehead (1983) utilized the concept of a cultural broker to facilitate the success of minority students in higher education. This concept can be expanded to facilitate the employment success of minorities with disabilities. Identification with one's own cultural group is important for social support as well as for one's own self-image. The ideal employment setting is one that does not down play selected cultures but tries to bridge the gap between various cultures.

Gentemann and Whitehead (1983) describe the concept of a cultural broker to convey the idea of links between the mainstream culture in a pluralistic society and the various ethnic cultures. The individual utilized as a cultural broker must understand the people, cultural symbols, and information from the various cultures and be able to communicate these values to each. The broker acts as an intermediary between cultures as well as the means by which individuals within the employment setting adapt to and adjust to each other.

46

Approach #3 Cross-Cultural Training

The provision of cross-cultural training within the work setting can be conducive to the continued employment of minority individuals with disabilities. Lee (1983) describes the necessity of cross-cultural training for Americans going abroad as well as those currently living in the United States so that persons can function with ease in the increasing multicultural society of America. Researchers have emphasized the problems and frustrations that individuals may encounter without cross-cultural training and knowledge of other cultures (Gentemann and Whitehead, 1983; Lee, 1983). Such an area of need and training can be expanded to include issues related to disability. The following suggestions are also offered which are aimed at improving the maintenance of employment for minority individuals with disabilities.

1. Increase the awareness of the American population so that people will know individuals with disabilities are able to be independent and self-sufficient (President's Committee on Employment of the Handicapped, 1986).

2. Increase individuals affirmation of the embracement of disabilities and cultural diversity within the American society.

3. Increase the awareness of employers and employees of the worth of individuals with disabilities.

4. Increase the awareness of employers and employees of cultural factors and the potential impact of such factors within the work setting.

SUMMARY

In summary, as the demographics shift, more minority individuals with disabilities will be needed to participate in the labor force. Changes within elementary, secondary, and post secondary institutions are needed in order to meet present as well as future needs within the labor force. Researchers have also indicated that the present vocational rehabilitation system does not sufficiently respond to the needs of and/or enhance the rehabilitation of minorities (Ross and Biggi, 1986). Therefore, changes are also needed within the vocational rehabilitation system. In view of the move from an industrial to a technological society, institutions of higher education must expand their efforts to increase the number and proportion of both able-bodied and nonable-bodied minority graduates.

All citizens should be educated to understand that minorities with disabilities have skills and the intellectual capacity which would enable them to achieve levels of social and economic worth. Employers and the vocational rehabilitation system must be encouraged to recruit, train and provide employment opportunities for minorities with disabilities as well as make the employment setting one that is conducive to cultural diversity. If America succeeds in encompassing the skills of all its members -- including minorities with disabilities -- all Americans will reap the benefits.

Footnote

1. Minority groups and/or minorities as used in this manuscript, refers to persons who are members of the following racial and ethnic groups as defined by the federal government: African Americans, Asian Americans, Native Americans, and Hispanics. It is acknowledged that in certain settings within the United States, members of the above groups may in fact constitute "the majority" population.

References

American Council on Education and the Education Commission of the States. (1988). A report on the commission on minority participation in education and American life: One-third of a Nation. Washington, DC: American Council on Education.

Banner, A.M. (1988). Towards effective independence: A goal for Black persons with disabilities in the United States. In S. Walker, J.W. Fowler, R.W. Nicholls & K.A. Turner (Eds.), Building bridges to independence: Employment successes, problems, and needs of Black Americans with disabilities. Proceedings of the national conference of the Howard University Model to Improve Rehabilitation Services to Minority Populations with Handicapping Disabilities. Washington, DC: The Center for the Study of Handicapped Children and Youth, School of Education, Howard University.

Beck, S.L. (1988). Career education for students with handicaps. Monographs Vol. 3(3). (ERIC Document Reproduction Service No. ED 301 758).

Collier, M., Ribeau, Sidney & Hecht, M. (1986). Intracultural communication rules and outcomes within three domestic cultures. International Journal of Intercultural Relations, 10, 439-457.

Gentemann, K.M. and Whitehead, T.L. (1983). The cultural broker concept in bicultural education. Journal of Negro Education, 52 (2), 118-129.

Johnson, W.B. et al. (1987). Workforce 2000: Work and Workers for the 21st Century. Indianapolis, IN: Hudson Institute.

Lee, Chris. (1983). Cross-cultural training: Don't leave home without it. Training, 20 (7), 20-25.

President's Committee on Employment of the Handicapped. (1985). Black adults with disabilities: A statistical report drawn from Census Bureau Data (Shipping list No. 85-1133-P; Item 766; MC #86-7133, SuDoc #1.10:B56). Washington, DC.

President's Committee on Employment of the Handicapped (1986). Out of the job market. (ERIC Document Reproduction Service No. ED 288 312). Washington, DC.

Ross, M.Gerlene and Biggi, Ian M. (1986). Critical vocational rehabilitation service delivery issues at referral (02) and closure (08, 26, 28, 30) in serving select disabled persons. In S. Walker, F.Z.Belgrave, A. M. Banner, & R.W. Nicholls (Eds.), Equal to the challenge: Perspectives, problems, and strategies in the rehabilitation of the nonwhite disabled. (Proceedings of the National Conference of the Howard University Model to Improve Rehabilitation Services to Minority Populations with Handicapping Conditions). Washington, DC: The Center for the Study of Handicapped Children and Youth, School of Education, Howard University.

Thorne, C.V. (1988). Effective approaches to education and economic independence for Black Americans with disabilities: A response. In S. Walker, et. al. (Eds.), Building bridges to independence: Employment success, problems, and needs of Black Americans with disabilities. (Proceedings of the National Conference of the Howard University Model to Improve Rehabilitation Services to Minority Populations with Handicapping). Washington, DC: The Center for the Study of Handicapped Children and Youth, School of Education, Howard University.

Walker, Sylvia (1984). Issues and trends in the education of the severely handicapped. In E. Gordon (Ed.), Annual review of research in education (Volume II). Washington, DC: American Education Research Association.

Walker, Sylvia (1988). Towards economic opportunity and independence: A goal for minority persons with disabilities. In, S. Walker, J.W. Fowler, R.W. Nicholls & K.A. Turner (Eds.), Building bridges to independence: Employment, successes, problems and needs of Black Americans with disabilities. Proceedings of the National Conference of the Howard University Model to Improve Rehabilitation Services to Minority Populations with Handicapping Conditions. Washington, DC: The Center for the Study of Handicapped Children and Youth, School of Education, Howard University.

HISPANICS WITH DISABILITIES IN THE LABOR FORCE: " A WINDOW OF OPPORTUNITY"

ANTONIO SUAZO
NATIONAL DISABILITY COORDINATOR
ACL-CIO RESOURCES DEVELOPMENT INSTITUTE

Abstract

This paper discusses the changing labor market as well as how the market is changing for Hispanics. Hispanic participation in the labor force will increase to ten percent by the year 2000. These labor market changes have implications for Hispanic persons with disabilities. Changes in the structure of work will also impact Hispanics with disabilities. Some of these changes include less physically demanding work, less dependence on job location and more flexibility for working at home away from the job-site, greater emphasis on service occupations, and greater emphasis on computer technology. In order to meet these labor market changes, Hispanics with disabilities have to be prepared. Programs to train bilingual, bicultural professionals are needed.

Organized labor has a long history of involvement with disability issues in this country. The most recent is the endorsement of the Americans with Disabilities Act (ADA) by the AFL-CIO. We see in the passage of this bill, the establishment of a level playing field for all Americans, including persons with disabilities. This paper provides an overview of the changing labor market followed by how the market is changing for Hispanics. Implications and recommendations for Hispanics with disabilities will be presented in the final section of the paper.

We currently hear a lot about Hispanics. The implication is that they are fairly recent to this country, but in fact, Hispanics have been in this country long before the Pilgrims landed at Plymouth Rock. St. Augustine, Florida, and Santa Fe, New Mexico--two of the oldest settlements in this country--were settled by Hispanics. In going over some family archives I noticed that my ancestors came with Coronado and settled in northern New Mexico in 1522 and that my grandfather served as a sergeant in the Union Army that fought in the Civil War. Some day we may have another movie entitled: "Gloria" portraying the role of Hispanics in the Civil War the way "Glory" depicted the role of Black soldiers in that war.

Labor Force Changes

Labor force changes are going to be far different by the next century from what it is today. It is in this changing labor market that people with disabilities will have to compete. Department of Labor studies report that the workforce will grow slowly, becoming older, more female and have more participants who are ethnic minorities. For example only 15 percent of new entrants to the labor force over the next 13 years will be native born, White males compared with 47 percent in that category today. Ethnic minorities will comprise one fourth of the labor force by the year 2000. During the last years of the 20th Century, immigrants will make up a larger share of the workforce.

The age of the labor force is also shifting, with younger and older workers comprising a smaller share of the labor force. More women than men will be entering the labor force. Most job growth will be in services and the retail trades, with the biggest increase occurring in the service industries, particularly health and business services. New jobs will demand a more skilled and highly educated work force.

Recently, I attended a forum on "older workers" on Capitol Hill and was impressed with reports that we are entering a period of labor shortages at all levels. The years of picky hiring are over, and vicious competition for all sorts of workers from entry-level to highly skilled has begun. The supply of new and older workers will dwindle in a time of rising demand for both. Many say that older workers need not retire early to create job opportunities for the young. There will be a demand for both. Yet in a recent survey most respondents felt that people over 65 should retire. Early retirement has been the trend both in Europe and in this country encouraged by both public policy and economic factors. There is, however, a dichotomy between the labor market trend towards early retirement and the anticipated labor shortages of the 21st Century. The conventional wisdom based on demographic data in this country now is that people should not have to retire because of age but should have the option of continuing to work if they want to.

Among the multitude of critically important workplace issues are:

o   Strong foreign competition

o   Rapid changes in technology

o   Inadequate education and job training systems

o   Rising health care costs, which are one of the most hotly contested issues in labor negotiations today.

Alternatives such as co-payment plans, and cheaper and less flexible plans are being advanced. The strikes at AT&T, the Regional Bell operating companies, and Pittston Coal all revolved around some aspect of runaway health care costs.

Labor Market Changes and Hispanics

These new developments and emerging market trends obviously will have a direct impact on minorities with disabilities. There is an old saying that "A rising tide raises all boats". This applies to all minorities. For Hispanics, the coming period will provide " a golden window of opportunity". Hispanic's participation in the labor force will rise from 4% in 1976 to 10% by the year 2000 -- for a 6% increase. This represents one of the largest increases by any group and will result in 6 million more Hispanics entering the labor force. By the year 2000, there will be a total of 14 million Hispanics in the labor force. What, then, are the implications of the changing labor market for persons with disabilities who come into the labor force with a Hispanics heritage.

First, let me briefly share a few figures with you.

o   Since 1980, the Hispanic population has grown by 39 percent.

o   The native Hispanic population is now 20.1 million or 8.2 percent of the total U.S. population. In the greater Washington-Baltimore area, there are currently over 350,000 Hispanics.

o   Demographic projections show that Hispanics will become the largest minority by the year 2025.

o   The 12.6 million Americans of Mexican origin are the largest Hispanic subgroup.

o   Over half (53.2 percent) of Hispanic women are currently in the labor force. This proportion is projected to grow to 57 percent by the year 2000, when 5.8 million women of Hispanic origin are expected to be in the labor force, bringing with them the problems of child care and elder care. Hispanic women are the fastest growing group of workers in the labor force, according to Bernice Friedlander, an official of the Women's Bureau at the Department of Labor.

o   This dramatic growth of Hispanics, of course translates into

        -       Economic and
        -       Political empowerment

        Among the highly visible signs of the growing Hispanic impact in this country are two Hispanic cabinet members with Secretary of Interior Manuel Lujan and Secretary of Education Lauro Cavazos, a first in the history of this country.

o   A Hispanic, Dr. Antonia Navellos has been appointed as Chief Medical Officer in the U.S.

o   The <u>Hispanic Legislative Caucus</u> is having a growing impact.

o   There has been the formulation of the Hispanic Chamber of Commerce and the growth of the Hispanic market. Hispanic affluence is also on the rise. Some <u>half a million Hispanic</u> households qualified as <u>affluent</u> in 1986, a 7% increase over 1980.

Yet, in some ways, trends in the Hispanic community seem to be in direct contrast to those for the rest of the country.

o   Hispanics are one of the fastest growing segments of the country, yet they have a smaller share of jobs, less education, and less skill training.

o   As the U.S. population grows older, Hispanics as a group remain comparatively young. At present the average age is 22 for Hispanics and 30 for non-Hispanics.

o   As the overall birth rate declines and the baby boomers reach middle age, Hispanics are maintaining a higher birth rate than any other group. At this rate, there will be a generation of "Hispanics baby boomers" in the years ahead.

o   As the suburbs grow, Hispanics tend to congregate in urban areas.

Yet, Hispanics have the same problems as other minorities. Disproportionate numbers are below the poverty line, have lower educational achievement and a high percentage are school dropouts.

A recent study released by Education Secretary Lauro F. Cavazos, reported the nation's dropout rate declined in the last decade. The disturbing fact was that, while dropout rates improved for both Black and White students, they remained the same for Hispanics. One recent theory is that this may be the result of a breakdown in family discipline rather than difficulties with language. Secretary Cavazos said, "For our Hispanic population, this is a national tragedy." In 1988, one-third of young adult Hispanics were not high school graduates.

The level of employment of Hispanics in the Federal government is particular disturbing. Hispanics made up <u>7.2</u> percent of the national workforce in 1988 but only constituted <u>5.2</u> percent of the federal workforce. A National Commission for Employment Policy (1990) report based on a 12-month study found that the Job Training Partnership Act (JTPA) needs some "fine tuning" to meet the needs of the Hispanic population. The report concluded that Hispanics continue to be the only minority group that shows <u>manifest imbalance</u> in the Federal work force. It recommended that elected officials make every effort to hire Hispanics especially for policy making positions when they are in a position to advocate and promote Hispanic involvement in JTPA. As someone said recently, "You would hope that if anyone is going to hire a workforce that is representative of our nation's ethnic make-up, it would be the federal government."

Impact of Labor Market Changes on Hispanics with Disabilities

The projected labor shortage in this country offers a "golden window of opportunity" for Hispanics in general and Hispanics with disabilities in particular. There is no one solution--no silver bullet to solve the problems of minorities with disabilities and the problems need to be attacked on many fronts, but there are many encouraging signs:

1. We are redefining the structure of work in this country.

2. The physical demands of jobs are decreasing -- over half of current jobs are automated, enabling the more severely disabled to compete. Many jobs are less arduous, we now have electronic mail, fax machines, and word processors. Computer technology has also led to less dependence on geographic locations. Work at home or close to home is much more feasible than it was a few year ago. Checkout scanners that trigger automatic orders for restocking will enable persons with disabilities to perform at a competitive level.

3. Emphasis and growth is on service occupations. Traditionally, this area of work offers good opportunities for people with disabilities.

4. Computer technology has opened up the employment market to persons with disabilities. Talking computers that respond to voice command, software that displays extra large type, and telecommunication devices have made the world more accessible to persons with disabilities. Information process is putting fax machines in cars and moving the workplace anywhere within reach of a telephone.

Preparing Hispanics with Disabilities for the Labor Force of the Future

Someone said (I believe it was Peter Drucker) that the best way to predict the future is to create it. And, that is the challenge we all face. The future workforce will include a proportionate share of minorities in the workforce if we can make it happen." From 1988 to the year 2000, nearly 43 million will enter the labor force, with 23 million replacing workers who retire or leave the labor force. We need to ensure that minorities with disabilities are as well prepared as anyone in order to compete. We need to assist them in developing high level skills and portable credentials to take with them when they change jobs. "Employers will hire competence wherever they find it." Minorities need to be prepared to compete in job growth areas. Business, health services and the retail trades will account for 9 more million jobs by the turn of the century.

For Hispanics, we need effective outreach programs to train bi-lingual, bi-cultural professionals in sufficient numbers to make an impact. And we need to consider the cultural factors impacting on Hispanics and the barriers they pose to employment. For example, a strong work ethic drives many to accept low-paying jobs rather than remain unemployed leading to exploitation. Strong family ties while providing group support can also cause absenteeism from work in times of family problems. Documentation for eligibility for public programs hinder participation. We need to accelerate the development of a national employment policy for minority persons who are disabled. There is clearly a need for public policy to address these issues. The working environment also needs to change. When you expect persons with disabilities to do all the adapting you sap them of their energy that could otherwise go into their work. The disability community needs to develop successful strategies to respond to the changing realities of the world of work.

It is generally agreed that we also need to examine the attitudes and belief systems of Hispanics. To be successful, Hispanics with disabilities along with other minorities, can emulate the efforts of others who have faced similar problems and have succeeded in their quest for opportunity.

References

Training Hispanics: Implications for the JTPA Systems. Washington, DC: National Commission for Employment Policy, January 1990.

Monthly Labor Review, Vol 110, No. 9 Washington, DC: U.S. Department , September 1987.

Workforce 2000, Washington, DC: U.S. Department of Labor, 1987.

Excellent at Work: The Issue. Washington, DC: National Governors Association, February 1990.

Hispanic Population Surpasses 20 Million Mark. Washington, DC: U.S. Department of Commerce, October 1989.

VOCATIONAL REHABILITATION AND THE AMERICAN INDIAN: WHERE IS THE INNOVATION?

JENNIE R. JOE
NATIVE AMERICAN RESEARCH AND TRAINING CENTER
UNIVERSITY OF ARIZONA

Abstract

Empowerment is important for persons with disabilities. In the American Indian community, empowerment is self-determination. This paper discusses some of the challenges to vocational rehabilitation programs in American Indian communities. Some of these challenges include under-funding for the vocational rehabilitation programs needed, lack of jobs in the community and lack of trained rehabilitation specialists. The paper also discusses how traditional occupations of American Indians can be used to increase employment and self-determination. One approach is to use the indigenous occupations and the talents of American Indians. The traditional tribal healer and artist are two examples of indigenous occupations that American Indians with disabilities can be trained in.

The theme of empowerment is important for persons with disabilities. One way to empower a person is to recognize and respect their cultural heritage. For example, to empower persons with disabilities is to give them a chance to provide for themselves and their families. Thus vocational rehabilitation (VR) is an important step toward taking off the "cloak of dependence." In American Indian communities, the most common term used to indicate empowerment is "self-determination."

Self-determination is especially important to American Indians because as a conquered people, they have had to endure various forms of genocide in addition to land dispossession and displacement onto unproductive reservation lands. There they have fallen into a cycle of poverty that has perpetuated a lifestyle of dependency, especially on the federal government. Today, this cycle of poverty and dependency continues despite a variety of government programs and congressional initiatives. This paper will discuss some of the challenges of providing VR to American Indians as well as settings in which traditional occupations can be used to facilitate successful rehabilitation.

Demographics on American Indians

According to the 1980 census, there are approximately 1.4 million persons in the United States who identify themselves as American Indians or Alaska Natives. This represents less than one percent of the total population. American Indians with disabilities, therefore, are a minority within a minority. Although American Indians are no longer confined to the reservation, most who leave the reservation and move into the cities maintain linkages with their tribal communities and thus also maintain a strong sense of their tribal identity.

From the standpoint of federal and other governmental entities, who is acknowledged as an American Indian is dependent on whether that person is part of a tribe that has federal or state recognition. That recognition is also dependent on the percentage of Indian blood. Generally a person with a quarter of more blood quantum qualifies as a tribal member. Today there are over 500 federally recognized tribes in the United States, and the list is growing as tribes which have not been recognized are petitioning for such recognition. Although Indian tribes are heterogeneous, they do share some things in common. For example, most have strong ties to the land and may share a world view that stresses harmony with nature.

The Role of the Traditional Tribal Healer

Within this context of harmony, is the tribal ethos regarding concepts of health, illness, disability, and/or misfortune. Thus in addition to modern medicine, many tribes continue to utilize their traditional healers. Indian clients with disabilities therefore also avail themselves of this resource when it is deemed necessary and helpful. The general understanding is that the treatment from a medicine person may not "cure" the disability, but the treatment may serve to help the individual and his/her family to understand "why" a disability occurred while the physician or other restorative measures respond to the question of "how" the disability occurred. The traditional healing resources for the persons with disabilities are significant because the traditional ceremonies conducted often help the client cope and/or regain a sense of well-being, empowering them to concentrate on restorative or rehabilitative endeavors. Because of the recognition that the need for and use of traditional tribal healers or medicine men is important, their use has been included in the 1986 reauthorization of the Rehabilitation Act.

Reservation - Based Vocational Rehabilitation

The Rehabilitation Act of 1978 expanded and provided American Indian tribes an opportunity to apply for federal funds in order to establish or explore the feasibility of establishing reservation-based vocational rehabilitation programs. This process leads to another way by which Indian people can become "empowered." Presently there are 14 such project operating. There are two such programs in Alaska, two in Arizona, three in Montana, two in Washington state, and one each in the states of New Mexico, Wyoming, Idaho, Oklahoma, and Colorado. The VR program serving the smallest tribe is that of the Yavapai Apache in Arizona; the large VR program is that of the Navajo Nation. According to a recent survey (Locust, 1990), the average case load for each of these programs varies from 30 to 1000 clients. The average age of the clients is 34 years, and slightly over half of the clients are males. As to rehabilitation services, the following table summaries the status of 1630 active clients presently being served by these projects:

STATUS	
In academic programs	20%
In vocational training	55%
In indigenous trade/crafts	1%
Other	24%
	100%

Those listed under "other" are clients who are either in the evaluation or the restorative phase of their vocational rehabilitation program.

Challenges In Providing Vocational Rehabilitation

The vocational rehabilitation programs on the Indian reservations face a multitude of challenges. First of all, their longevity is very precarious. These projects must re-apply and compete every three years for funding. Most are severely under-funded and their ability to help clients is also hampered by the fact that most rural communities where they are located have chronic high unemployment, which ranges between 50 to 80% in some communities. Thus the VR client must compete for the few jobs available against a waiting list of many unemployed "able-bodied." Thus in addition to general vocational rehabilitation counseling, many of the counselors must also concern themselves with job development.

Another major problem facing these new VR programs in Indian communities, is the lack of trained manpower in rehabilitation, especially counseling, vocational evaluation, and administration. Further compounding these problems is the fact that the concept of vocational rehabilitation is still relatively unknown to most American Indians and Alaska Natives, despite the fact that vocational training has historically been forced on Indians as part of the efforts to "mainstream" them into the majority culture. Many of the VR clients have had little or no opportunity to have "meaningful" employment because of numerous barriers, and thus one of their first positive experiences with the workplace environment may occur as a client in the VR program.

Most clients with disabilities have had spotty employment opportunities and do not enter the system as a result of referrals associated with employment. Most of them enter the VR process as a result of disabilities associated with accidents, usually automobile accidents. Others may be referred as a result of learning disabilities which have limited their chances to learn a job skill. Others may have a disability as a result of complications stemming from infectious diseases or conditions such as non-insulin dependent diabetes mellitus. Diabetes is one of the major health problems among many tribes, and various secondary complications such as amputation, vision loss, or renal failure are becoming increasingly common among the employable age group.

Although VR program staff try to be flexible and innovative in their approach, many find their programs criticized by state VR people for what these officials perceive as a failure to deliver "quality" or "standard" vocational rehabilitation services. Unfortunately, the state programs do not realize that most of the Indian VR programs do not have the infrastructure or financial resources to provide many of the "standard" services. For example, the Indian VR projects do not have separate funding to help provide inservice or other training programs for their staff. They also generally do not have the funds to pay adequate salaries for their counselors.

Unfortunately, as these Indian VR programs try to model themselves after the "standard" VR services, they must also produce successful closures, i.e., clients who have been successfully placed in a wage earning position. Thus to some extent, programs are forced to take the cases that are most likely to succeed and those more difficult cases most in need of rehabilitation services may go lacking. This "creaming" approach is difficult for some community members, especially those with severe disabilities, to understand.

As the "new kids on the VR block," many of the Indian VR programs also must demonstrate their success as a typical VR program by preparing and placing clients in the type of occupations or work situations that are acceptable to the general vocational rehabilitation programs such as blue collar jobs. By placing priority on such job development, these Indian VR programs are forced to overlook or not give priority to indigenous occupations. For example, although most tribes lament the passing of some of their traditional crafts and specialists such as herbalists, healers, weavers, artists, and/or language teachers, few VR counselors encourage clients to explore these fields. If they did, the outcome might lead to re-establishing some of these traditional occupations as well as providing much needed employment.

Alternate Approaches to VR

The indigenous occupations and the talents that still exist among many tribes indicate the economic feasibility as well as the tremendous pride that these artists, for example, take in producing their one-of-a-kind works of art. The products they produce allow them to be innovative as well as give them the opportunity to experiment. One role model among the Indians in the southwest who illustrates this principle is Michael Naranjo from Santa Clara Pueblo. Michael is blind but nevertheless produces award winning artwork that is in great demand by many collectors.

Similarly there are many healer who have been disabled but whose services have always been in great demand. Because of the advent of mandatory education for Indian children, very few young people now enter the practice of healing. The Indian VR programs could help change this trend by allowing apprenticeships with traditional healers of clients who are interested and are acceptable. Similarly, the encouragement of clients to develop skills and expertise in tribal language would enable them to teach young children traditional language, music, and other skills and arts.

These are but a few suggestions of possible innovations for the Indian VR client, and ways in which to make VR more responsive to the needs of the culture groups whom they serve. Historically, minority participation in VR has not been significant, and allowing groups such as American Indians to develop VR services for their population is an encouraging way to increase the participation of minorities in the VR process. These programs must also receive adequate support as well as the encouragement to be innovative. They should be allowed to utilize the strengths of their culture so that they can better realize self-determination or empowerment.

Reference

Locust, Carol (1990) Personnel communication. Tucson, Arizona.

THE EMPLOYMENT OF ASIAN/PACIFIC MINORITY PERSONS WITH DISABILITIES

ALAN H. WOO
ASIAN REHABILITATION SERVICES

Abstract

It is vitally important that ethnic minorities consider the role they are to play in reshaping the nature of work and the workplace. The workplace still reflects the White male value system. Ethnic minorities are uncomfortable in this environment. The challenge is to change the workplace so that minority persons with disabilities are welcome and given equal work. The number of Asian/Pacific persons with disabilities is growing rapidly. The number being served by the California State Department of Rehabilitation is not in proportion to the population. Barriers to success include difficulties in cultural transitioning; family systems differences; language differences; lack of culturally relevant assessment tools; inappropriate rehabilitation techniques and services; differences in cultural values, beliefs, and practices; and a lack of training of a culturally sensitive and linguistically appropriate staff. The Asian Rehabilitation Services, Inc. of Los Angeles provides a variety of services to overcome many of the above listed barriers. A thirteen point plan is recommended to help overcome cultural and language barriers and in turn provide meaningful work for minorities with disabilities in the future.

As the year 2000 approaches, it is vitally important that ethnic minorities, consider the role they are to play in reshaping the nature of work and the workplace. Women and ethnic minorities comprise 75% of the nation's workforce. The Western European male dominated corporate model will have to change. The workforce will be diverse. The future is already here.

Our growing numbers hold the key to the future. In many communities, ethnic minorities constitute the majority population. These communities are filled with ethnic minority restaurants, community institutions, cultural centers, small businesses, etc. However, for the most part, the workplace still reflects the White male value system. Ethnic minorities are uncomfortable in that environment.

If our goal is to simply create work for every minority person with a disability, then, it would be a rather simple task. The Chinese Emperors developed the following model: round up all the poor, and have them build a great wall for the next ten years. This will keep them busy and will keep them out of public view. However, I am haunted by a statement made by one of my clients at my workshop. He said: "I work hard in the workshop and get paid $20.00 for two weeks work. I don't think that's right, do you?" No, it is not right. But this is the real world we have created for persons with disabilities. It is also our challenge to change the workplace so that not only

62

individuals with disabilities are welcome and given equal work, but, minority persons with disabilities are welcome and given equal work. Government cannot provide the solution. Government solutions are similar to the example of the great wall. So, how can the workplace be changed? A few trends are discussed below.

<u>The Asian/Pacific Population on the West Coast</u>

From 1980 to 1988, the Asian/Pacific population grew at an average rate of 6.6% per year, thus, doubling the Asian/Pacific population nationally. In California, by the year 2000, Asian/Pacifics will be 12% of the state's population and 30% of the Los Angeles County population. In the Los Angeles area, Asian/Pacifics grew by 92% thus, making it the county with the largest concentration of Asian/Pacifics in the nation. The largest concentration of the Asian Pacific population in Los Angeles is foreign born, recent immigrants, with little or no English speaking skills.

The Asian/Pacific community is comprised of twenty-eight ethnic groups with diverse cultures and languages. The ten largest groups are: Cambodians, Chinese, Japanese, Korean, Filipino, Laotian, Thai, Tongan, Samoan, and Vietnamese.

In the Los Angeles area, population diversity is increasing with high rates of immigration and higher birth rates among racial and ethnic minorities. Seventy-five percent of all births in the Los Angeles area are Hispanic, African American, or Asian/Pacific. On the West Coast, this swelling growth and diversity have caused us to respond to changing and varying needs with greater understanding and flexible solutions. Thus, the demand for data and culturally sensitive services becomes a critical element to preparing Asian/Pacific persons with disabilities for work. There is very little data available regarding the numbers of Asian/Pacific persons with disabilities. But we do know that the numbers of Asian/Pacific persons with disabilities currently being served by the California State Department of Rehabilitation is not in proportion to the population. For example, in 1989, the State Department of Rehabilitation served 130,925 clients, of which, 60% (78,808) were White and only 3% (5,024) were Asian/Pacific. Yet, Asian/Pacifics are 12% of the state population and 30% of the Los Angeles area population. The Asian/Pacific population is being underserved.

This is largely due to the unfamiliarity of Asian/Pacifics with social services and because traditionally, most Asian/Pacifics do not seek help. Individuals with disabilities of families are usually hidden away and sometimes not registered in the family records. Also, culture and language barriers inhibit the use of available services. Most employers are reluctant to hire individuals with disabilities with limited English speaking skills. This points to a critical need for support services for newcomers. Culturally sensitive and linguistically appropriate outreach workers, job placement and job developers are needed to help place the limited English speaking persons with disabilities. The employers have to be willing to establish working enclaves of limited English speaking individuals with disabilities. For example, the Bank of America established a supported employment enclave of Cantonese speaking developmentally disabled and chronically mentally ill clients. They are supervised by a Cantonese speaking job coach reporting to a Cantonese speaking Bank of America supervisor. The clients feel more welcomed and accepted because they can communicate with co-workers while developing job skills and earning a living.

Most people think that the Asian/Pacific community is well educated and well off. The fact is that 12% of the Asian/Pacific population lives below the poverty level. Often persons with disabilities require additional support services that is difficult for traditional rehabilitation facilities to provide. For example, many of our families do not own cars, thus, our counselors have to visit potential clients and their families at their home, community centers, schools, or at other Asian/Pacific service agencies. In addition, the family often requires assistance to access other services such as resolving immigration problems, finding employment, rent assistance, cultural transition services, family counseling, family abuse intervention and prevention, and family strengthening services.

BARRIERS TO SUCCESS

The most prominent barriers include difficulties in cultural transitioning; differences in values of family systems; language differences; lack of culturally relevant assessment tools, rehabilitation techniques and services; differences in cultural values, beliefs, and behaviors; inadequate service delivery systems; inadequate cultural sensitivity training; and not enough linguistically appropriate staff.

Cultural Values, Beliefs and Practices

"There is a very bad fit between the kind of services Americans might respond to in a crises and those needed by new immigrant populations with a whole set of beliefs and ways of seeking solace," said Elinore Lurie, Executive Director of the Mental Health Association of San Francisco. Lurie and others fear the same bad fit will keep a rapidly growing population of ethnic minorities in the state from getting appropriate mental health services as long as a shortage of bicultural and bilingual therapists persist. "What's fairly clear is that the mental health system has to change in order to accommodate itself to different kinds of people who are becoming the majority population in the state of California," said Steve Shon, Assistant Director for the State Department of Mental Health.

In many of the Asian/Pacific cultures, disability is viewed as destiny or a condition ordained by spirits or the Gods. In Northern California, a child with a disability was prevented from getting a simple clubfoot operation because the local shaman said that the spirits will be disturbed and this will bring bad fortune to the family. In Japanese culture, you keep persons with disabilities away from public view. Due to the Confucian emphasis on perfection, Chinese and Koreans are usually ashamed of their children with disabilities and do not record their birth in family records. Also, many Asian/Pacific cultures rely on herbal medicine, acupuncture, the Tao, and other non-Western approaches for healing. In mental health, Western methods do not work. In the East, different references are used.

Family Systems and Language

Asian/Pacifics place great emphasis on filial piety, family, and responsibility to the group. The work ethic is very strong. This helps to produce a very loyal, motivated, and dependable workforce. However, families are also overly protective. While most families will accept placing their children in a vocational rehabilitation workshop, they are reluctant to have their children work in the community. Parents fear that their children may be the subject of ridicule, get hurt, or get lost. For parents of the physically challenged, the disability is a constant reminder of failure and bad fortune. This also serves to lower the potential for marriage for the children without a disability. Often, parents will not acknowledge that they have offspring with disabilities. Also, women with disabilities are not encouraged to marry or to leave the house. To deal with the complexities of cultural influences and language barriers, bicultural and bilingual professionals are needed. These professionals understand the underlying traditional beliefs, and family structures, and can communicate in the appropriate language.

The Asian/Pacific community is comprised of many cultures, ethnic groups, and languages. For example service providers often need more than one Asian/Pacific specialist to cover the major ethnic groups. In the Los Angeles areas, there are several language groups including: Chinese (Mandarin and Cantonese), Japanese, Korean, Tagalog, Tongan, Cambodian, Thai, Vietnamese, and Laotian. Moreover, the problem is complicated in that services are only available in the traditional areas where early immigrants were concentrated such as Chinatown, Koreantown, Filipinotown, or Little Tokyo. However, in recent years, Asian/Pacifics have been moving in large numbers to surrounding cities. For example, in the City of Monterey Park, Asian/Pacifics are 75% of the city's population. The City has a Chinese Mayor, Chinese Councilman, and a Filipino Councilman. Yet, there are no social services available to our Asian/Pacific community.

Need for Service Providers

Although most service providers in the Los Angeles area are sensitive to the needs of the Asian Pacific community, there is not a sufficient pool of trained professionals to fill the demand. Most agencies hire one Asian/Pacific rehabilitation counselor and expect this person to serve all the different ethnic groups while also servicing a full load of other clients. Administrators don't realize that a Japanese counselor cannot speak Tagalog or Korean. Most of the professionals that are working for the Department of Rehabilitation and the Department of Mental Health have been trained and work at Asian Rehabilitation Services.

Overcoming the Barriers

In the early seventies, Asian/Pacific community leaders noticed that there were no services available to Asian/Pacific persons with disabilities. Also, there were no alternatives to institutionalization. Moreover, many Asian/Pacific developmentally disabled clients were misdiagnosed and placed in mental health hospitals because no one could communicate with them. The community organized and created Asian Rehabilitation Services, Inc (ARS). This model program provides vocational rehabilitation services to adult residents of Los Angeles County who are developmentally, emotionally, and/or physically disabled. ARS offers a wide variety of vocational, educational, personal development, and community services with special sensitivity to cultural and linguistic needs of Asian/Pacific and Spanish speaking persons with disabilities. Over the years, ARS has become the centralized case manager for Asian/Pacific disabled persons seeking job skills training, work experience, and job placement. ARS offers ESL and Vocational classes to clients who also are undergoing work experience programs. Services are offered in Mandarin, Cantonese, Tagalog, Japanese, Korean, and Spanish. ARS works with local regional centers, Department of Rehabilitation, Department of Mental Health, residential centers, Department of Social Services, and Asian/Pacific service agencies to place potential clients in the ARS program or in supported employment in the community.

ARS has also developed a promising private sector business model which is used to expand supported employment opportunities. Graduates of ARS Janitorial Training Program are found work in the private sector. ARS have also been successful in securing contracts to clean office buildings from which they can hire graduates from their training program directly. Thus, limited English speaking disabled graduates can still receive support services. Also, ARS is looking into the temporary factory help field and housekeeping for the Hotel industry to secure additional employment opportunities for its clients.

RECOMMENDATIONS

The following recommendations are made to help overcome cultural and language barriers so that meaningful work for minorities with disabilities can be provided in the future:

o   Encourage Asian/Pacific community groups to organize and demand culturally sensitive and bilingual services.

o   Emphasize participation of Asian/Pacifics in research, training and service delivery.

o   Conduct research and disseminate information for policy makers and service providers to better understand cultural differences. Respect the need to set up separate but equal programs of centralized services for Asian/Pacific persons with disabilities.

o   Train and hire more bilingual Asian/Pacific professionals.

o   Work with employers to change the workplace to enable it to be more inviting to the diverse ethnic community.

67

o   Duplicate the ARS model wherever possible. It is cost effective.

o   Continue research to determine the true prevalence of disability among the Asian/Pacific population and to develop culturally appropriate assessment tools.

o   Encourage major employers to develop special affirmative hiring programs for Asian/Pacific persons with disabilities.

o   Assist small business in hiring Asian/Pacific persons.

o   Develop a better service delivery system and rehabilitation program that is based on cultural diversity and that do not favor Anglo-Americans.

o   Hire culturally sensitive Asian/Pacific professionals in management positions who have power to make change.

o   Provide financial funding for community outreach and community education programs. This is the only way the community can be reached.

o   Increase transitional activities, eg., school-to-work, school-to-rehabilitation agency-to-work.

FUTURE FRONTIERS

FRONTIERS IN ASSISTIVE TECHNOLOGY

FUTURE FRONTIERS IN THE ACCESS TO TECHNOLOGY

ROBERT W. NICHOLLS
HOWARD UNIVERSITY RESEARCH AND TRAINING CENTER

Abstract

This article includes a comparison of two case studies of individuals with physical disabilities, one a tailor who lost his arm in an accident and the other a doctoral candidate in computer science who was born without arms. The experiences of these individuals indicate that many job opportunities related to the "Information Age" are available to individuals with disabilities as opposed to jobs that require manual dexterity. Many individuals who have a disability, because of specialization and limited accessibility as well as cost of many current technological devices, cannot afford the technology that could lead to independence in the job market. With information about new assistive technologies, individuals with disabilities will be able to explore this area to discover which enabling technology will work best for them in various settings.

Before I came to Howard University I was in Nigeria, there I had a friend who was a tailor. He had an accident, as a result his left was arm amputated. This was a traumatic experience. He had to have a series of operations because the amputation wouldn't heal properly and his arm was getting shorter and shorter. Eventually he was left with a stump just below the shoulder. Following the amputation he had to leave the relatively large town where he had worked as a tailor, to return to his village in the countryside to depend, at least initially, on the charity of his family. He could no longer pursue his profession as a tailor with just one arm. As I say, he was a friend of mine, therefore, in consultation with his family, it was decided that the best we could do for him at the time was to get him an artificial arm. This served cosmetic purposes--the prosthesis made him look more like he had looked before, but he couldn't really use it effectively, at least not as a tailor.

My Nigerian friend may be compared with an individual who was featured in the October, 1988 issue of the Howard University Center's Newsletter (Nicholls, 1988). He was a doctoral candidate in computer science at George Washington University who was born without arms, as an infant he had learned to use his feet with dexterity. As a result, he was able to operate the computer keyboard with his toes. He was very successful at designing software and constructing computer models. He won a national competition sponsored by Achievement Rewards for College Scientists (ARCS) whereby he was selected as the top science graduate student in the country. This was not a competition for people with disabilities. Furthermore, his disability was unknown to the people who selected him. He was competing on an equal basis with able-bodied people and he won.

I think it is relevant to juxtapose these two situations, remembering that we are now in the so-called "Information Age." This phrase is not used frequently now, but nevertheless that is where we are. Many of the jobs available, even apart from computer programming, involve the storage or communication of information in one form or another. Thus, this state of affairs has created opportunities for individuals with disabilities. The comparison of these two individuals informs us not so much about the differences between Nigeria and the U.S.A., but about the employment status of people with disabilities vis a vis the job market in an information economy. If, for example, my friend who lost his arm had been an information worker, an academic, a teacher, an accountant, a journalist, or something of that nature, his accident would not have had the devastating effect on his career. However, since his profession as a tailor created considerable physical demands requiring a degree of manual dexterity, the loss of his arm cut short his future in that particular occupation.

In previous work which I have conducted, I explored some of the problems of new assistive technology relative to cost, availability, and access to various technological devices (Nicholls, 1986). Many of the new devices have an enormous enabling potential. However, since they are new, specialized and aimed at a somewhat limited market they tend to be somewhat expensive. This creates a Catch-22 situation for many individuals with disabilities because they cannot afford the technology that could lead to independence and lucrative employment. The employment would in turn provide the financial resources that would pay for the appropriate technology. This creates a dilemma.

Dr. Sushila Kapur, who has an extensive orthopedic disability, points out the importance of economic status to persons with disabilities (Kapur, 1986). Rehabilitation and Government entitlements can only pay so much. She says that every time she turns around something is breaking down. She has an Amigo, a mechanical tricycle that she uses to get around. When the trunk lift in her car fails to work, she has to take a day off work to get it repaired. This eats into her sick leave or annual leave and in addition she has to pay a couple of hundred dollars to get the equipment repaired. The corollary seems to be that you have to be comparatively wealthy to have

71

technology. This does not bode well for people with disabilities, who tend to be among the less well-off in our society. Thus, many persons with disabilities need employment which will permit them to afford and maintain appropriate assistive technology.

The Howard University Research and Training Center will be making a series of videotapes of various technologies that provide "user friendly" information about new assistive technology. Very often, technology and information about technology tends to have a numbing effect. The descriptions and specifications are just too technical. However, if you can see the technology in operation or hear somebody who uses it talk about it and show you how it works, technology becomes a lot easier to understand. Our videotapes will show the use of technology in action and the way in which a particular individual with a disability is making a technology work for him/her in an educational, employment, or home environment. With new information about assistive technologies, individuals with disabilities and service providers will be able to explore this area to discover which enabling technology works best in a particular setting.

References

Kapur, S.(1986) Non-traditional career approaches for disabled non-white persons. In S. Walker, et al. (Eds.), Equal to the challenge: Perspectives, problems and strategies in the rehabilitation of the non-white disabled. Washington, D.C.: Bureau of Educational Research, Howard University.

Nicholls, Robert W. (1986). "New assistive technology and the nonwhite disabled." In S. Walker, et al. (Eds.), Equal to the challenge: Perspectives, problems, and strategies in the rehabilitation of the non-white disabled. Washington, DC: Howard University.

Nicholls, Robert W. (1988). "Graduate student with disability selected as top science graduate, "The Collaborative Model to Facilitate the Employment Success of Disabled Minority Persons: Newsletter (Howard University) Vol. 1. No. 2.

HEARING TO READ: THE KURZWEIL READING MACHINES

GRACE J. LYONS
DISTRICT OF COLUMBIA REGIONAL LIBRARY
FOR THE BLIND AND PHYSICALLY HANDICAPPED

Abstract

This article focuses on the use of the Kurzweil Reading Machine (KRM); This machine enables individuals with visual or reading disabilities to access printed text. Speed of delivery varies from 120 to 350 words per minute. An important feature of the device include spelling of the word(s). Materials read by the KRM can be loaded on a computer disk to be used later. The KRM can also load materials onto an audio cassette for listening at a later date.

Background

The first Kurzweil Reading Machine (KRM) was purchased by the District of Columbia Library for the Blind and Physically Handicapped in 1981 after our staff participated in a demonstration of the KRM presented by Raymond Kurzweil at the Veteran's Administration in Washington, D.C. Back in the 1970's while attending a conference of regional librarians in West Virginia, our staff visited the local rehabilitation center that had one of the original Kurzweils. It was the size of a small car and although we could not understand a single word, we were excited to witness the print turned into audio. We believed in the potential importance of this new technology.

We have trained over 100 persons to use the Kurzweil Reading Machine. Young children learn best in two's, one child reinforcing the other's understanding. We have trained electrical engineers who lost their sight in accidents. They were able to learn the KRM in one half hour. Usually the training takes from six to eight hours. The people who are most demanding of the technology take the longest to learn because they want to learn everything. Others get a general knowledge which you hope they will remember. People who are most serious need the most training. It is important to note that our library did not purchase the KRM to provide all of our readers with an in-house capability that serves all reading needs. We could never meet this goal. We intend to train readers on the KRM. Many have gone on to either purchase their own, or use one in their work place or school.

<u>The Kurzweil Opens Doors</u>

The Regional Library has recently ordered the new model, the Kurzweil Personal Reader (KPR) with hand scanner and automatic page scanner. It retails for about $12,000. I have seen it demonstrated. The computer and hand scanner weigh about 20 pounds; the automatic scanner is not truly portable. This machine offers a choice of nine different narrator voices which give variation in long term reading. Speed of delivery varies from 120 to 350 words per minute. The hand scanner is guided across the page by a magnetic sheet which is inserted under the page to be read.

In addition to visually impaired individuals, persons with reading disabilities can also benefit from using the KPR, because it not only reads a word, it also spells. Thus a person with a reading disability can read a book while listening to it on the KRM at the same time (he/she would need two copies of the book). The new KPR is computer compatible. Materials read by the KPR can be loaded onto a computer disk which can be taken by the reader to be read on another computer with voice output. This is an important advantage for persons doing research. The KPR can also load materials read, onto an audio cassette for listening at a later date. The new KPR learns the type font in seconds. This is important particularly for young readers who are impatient.

In closing, the adaptability and intelligence of our visually impaired clientele must be emphasized. Many of them run their own businesses using computers. Clients are often referred to one another when our resources run out. In fact, our readers are our most important resources.

Bibliography

Bowe, Frank G. (1984). <u>Personal computers and special needs</u>. Berkley, SYBEX.

McWilliams, Peter A. (1984). <u>Personal computers and the disabled</u>. Garden City, New York, Quantum Press (Doubleday).

National Library Service for the Blind and Physically Handicapped/Library of Congress. (September, 1987). <u>Facts: Computer technology for handicapped persons</u>.

WHAT IS APPROPRIATE TECHNOLOGY?

JAN GALVIN
BETSY PHILLIPS
REQUEST REHABILITATION ENGINEERING CENTER
NATIONAL REHABILITATION HOSPITAL

Abstract

This article emphasizes the fact that recent legislation has created new opportunities for improving the quality of life for individuals with disabilities through the application of technology in the work environment. The application of assistive technology involves a logical problem solving process. Appropriate interventions may range from compensatory strategies to simple adaptive aids to sophisticated computerized devices. If consumers and professionals work together and follow basic principles of selection, more successful outcomes will result.

Background

The potential of technology to help persons with disabilities achieve maximum independent functioning is well recognized in rehabilitation. Several pieces of legislation have created new opportunities for persons with disabilities to use technology in improving their quality of life. Section 508 of the Rehabilitation Reauthorization Act of 1986 requires that all federal agencies provide equivalent access to all electronic office equipment (i.e., computers) for all persons regardless of disability. The Technology-Related Assistance for Individuals with Disabilities Act of 1988 provides funding for grants to states to develop comprehensive statewide consumer responsive delivery systems for rehabilitation engineering and assistive technology services. Lastly, the Americans with Disabilities Act (ADA) prohibits discrimination against persons with disabilities in private sector employment, transportation, public services and accommodations and telecommunications. This heightened interest in and awareness of technology is encouraging, but there is cause for caution. When you hear the word "technology," what comes to mind? You may think of talking computers, robots, laser optics, and spy satellites, but probably not door levers, canes, telephone headsets, or job sharing. We often assume that "bigger, newer, and more sophisticated" means better. Therefore, we tend to look to high technology solutions for every situation. This myopic view of assistive technology must be broadened. Our excitement over high technology must be tempered by realism. High technology is often expensive, difficult to maintain and requires extensive training to use (PSI International, 1985). Low technology alternatives can be just as effective and more easily integrated into a person's lifestyle. Appropriate technology interventions occur at all levels of technology and can be achieved through the implementation of a logical, systematic decision-making approach, guided by certain fundamental principles. However, it is important to have a clear understanding of what "assistive technology" is before examining its appropriateness.

Assistive Technology - Definitions

The terminology regarding technology-related assistance for persons with disabilities has developed over the years. Two key concepts are central to current thinking about technology: 1) Technology is a **process** that involves the application of scientific knowledge to practical purposes, and 2) assistive technology is the use of **compensatory strategies** and **adaptive equipment** to increase, improve or maintain capabilities of individuals with disabilities. This includes, but is not limited to, the use of equipment, hardware, information, procedures, and adaptive compensatory strategies (Corthell, 1986). The comprehensive definitions of assistive technology complement the principles described below.

Appropriate Assistive Technology

Appropriate assistive technology is unique for each person and can be achieved through the application of a comprehensive, flexible, and logical problem-solving process. This process is guided by certain basic principles that, if followed, can result in more successful outcomes.

Work Together. Consumers and professionals need to work together to obtain the best outcomes. Consumers bring expertise to the rehabilitation process - intimate knowledge of their personal values, goals, priorities, attitudes toward technology, home and community environment and support systems. Professionals are knowledgeable about the types of technology on the market, their applications, and how to match specific technology with a consumer's functional abilities. All of these factors are important to the integration of assistive technology into the consumer's lifestyle and must be considered in selecting technology (Cook, 1982; Scherer & McKee,

1989; Zola, 1982).

Focus on Function. A thorough evaluation of the consumer's functional abilities must be conducted. At the same time, the functional requirements of tasks that the consumer will be doing (be it at home, work, or community) need to be analyzed. Searching for technology that will augment the consumer's positive, usable functions enables him/her to complete designated tasks (McFarland, 1984).

Individualize Solutions. It is easy to fall into the trap of recommending or requesting products that have worked for others. The tendency to rely on familiar equipment must be resisted since other more appropriate products or strategies may be overlooked. A "one size fits all" philosophy is the antithesis of good technology-related assistance. Every person's needs are unique, so technological solutions must be individualized accordingly.

Keep It Simple. Choose technology that meets specific, targeted needs. The most complicated machines are not necessarily the most appropriate and may be more difficult to use and repair. Avoid choosing equipment that has extra "bells and whistles," features that add to costs, but will likely go unused. Remember, keep it simple. Select interventions that will ensure that the use of assistive devices is not overshadowed by the technology itself. Assistive devices should not make a person so independent that the need for human interaction is eliminated. Remember, keep it human.

Be Holistic. Technology does not exist in a vacuum; always consider the whole picture when evaluating technological needs. Environmental, personal, and sociopsychological aspects of the intervention must be considered, as well as the functional aspects. These elements can influence the successful use and retention of the chosen device (Vash, 1983). For example, technology cannot replace basic job skills and qualifications. Technological applications that enable access to a computer cannot substitute for word processing knowledge. If a person has the necessary training and skills to perform a job, then technology can often provide the physical means to assist the employee to complete the required tasks.

Furthermore, adaptations that severely inconvenience a consumer's co-workers may strain work relationships. On the other hand, interventions that can be generalized will enhance the job performance of all employees. For example, a standard telephone headset can often be used by persons with limited hand function to answer telephones. Others in the office who answer telephones can also benefit from this device since it prevents repetitive motion disorders such as frozen shoulder, and frees their hands for other tasks. Well thought out technology solutions can benefit everyone involved.

Choose the Least Invasive Alternative. The following hierarchy of technology intervention strategies provides a guide from simplest to most complex solutions. The steps in the hierarchy are:

o   modify or adapt the task when possible (restructuring of tasks, activities, and the environment to compensate for functional limitations including architectural modifications, attendant care arrangements and job restructuring);

o   select devices from among commercially available products;

o   utilize commonly available products in creative ways (for example, telephone headsets and dictaphones);

o   combine technologies not typically used together (operating a voice controlled environmental control unit with a walkie-talkie);

o   modify existing commercial devices;

o   design and fabricate a new device.

Compensatory strategies should be considered first because they are generally simple and of low cost. For example, altering a 9-5 job to flextime and rearranging the office may be all that is required to enable an employee to return to work. Fabrication of a new device is the last resort because it may take a long time to construct, can be more expensive due to labor costs, and may be difficult to repair or update due to its uniqueness.

Whichever option is selected, try to "test drive" it prior to making a final decision. If the solution does not seem to be viable, do not be afraid to go back to the beginning and redefine the problem. At least you have discovered a problem before a purchase is made. Money for assistive technology services is limited, therefore, careful consideration of all options is necessary to select the most effective solution for a particular individual.

The application of these basic principles during the selection process, will likely result in more appropriate and successful assistive technology interventions. The Request Rehabilitation Engineering Center on the Evaluation of Technology at the National Rehabilitation Hospital can provide more information in this area. Additional information and resources on a variety of topics related to assistive technology are available.

References

Cook, A.M. (1982). Delivery of assistive devices through a client-oriented approach. In M.R. Redden & V.W. Stern (Eds.), Technology for Independent Living (pp. 29-31). Washington, D.C.: American Association for the Advancement of Science.

Corthell, D.W. (Ed). (1986). Thirteenth institute on rehabilitation technologies. Menomonie, Wisconsin: University of Wisconsin-Stout, Research and Training Center.

McFarland, S.R. (1984). Technology at the workplace. In A. Enders (Ed.), Technology for Independent Living Sourcebook (pp. 85-88). Washington, DC: RESNA.

PSI International, Inc. (1985). Low-cost technology (Rehab Brief, Vol. VIII, No. 1). Falls Church, VA: Author.

Scherer, M.J. & McKee B.G. (1989). But will the assistive technology device be used? In J.J. Presperin (Ed.), Proceedings of the 12th Annual Conference of the Rehabilitation Engineering Society of North America (pp. 356-357). Washington, DC: RESNA Press.

Vash, C.L. (1983). Psychological aspects of rehabilitation engineering. In M.R. Redden & V.W. Stern (Eds.), Technology for Independent Living II: Issues in Technology for Daily Living, Education, and Employment (pp. 48-59). Washington, DC: American Association for the Advancement of Science.

Zola, I.K. (1982). Involving the consumer in the rehabilitation process: Easier said than done. In M.R. Redden & V.W. Stern (Eds.), Technology for Independent Living (pp. 112-121). Washington, DC: American Association for the Advancement of Science.

THE COMPUTER: A VEHICLE FOR ACCESS FOR PEOPLE WITH DISABILITIES

SUSAN BOAZ
DEPARTMENT OF VETERANS AFFAIRS

Abstract

The author defines computer accommodation as any device used in conjunction with a computer to eliminate an employee's functional limitations and permit access to a computer. In an employment setting, computers should accommodate individual needs and/or focus on particular limitation(s). Many devices facilitate full access to a computer. Such technologies include telecommunications for the hearing impaired, glare protection screen for the visually impaired and many keyboard alternatives input devices such as Morse Code for motor impaired individuals. Training programs are beneficial as they enable an individual to optimize use of equipment. Involving the person with disabilities in the decision making process is of importance in providing appropriate training and meeting individual needs.

A computer accommodation is any aid, device or service which eliminates an employee's functional limitations and permits access to a computer. For example, I am blind and in order for me to use a computer, it either has to speak to me or it has to give me braille because I use braille a lot. Basically, the computer must do one of those two things. Otherwise, I do not know what the computer is doing. The functional limitation in my case is lack of vision. However, there are access solutions out there such as Braille 'N Speak which costs about $900. It is a little computer in and of itself. I can take notes with it. It is almost like a shorthand system or a court-reporting system. After I have finished taking notes I can go home and hook it up with a regular computer, load the files into my big system, do some fancy editing and come out with a good report. The Braille 'N Speak device weighs less than a pound. I find it useful to have a nice portable computer. There are many solutions out there; and we are going to discuss some of them. With regards to computer accommodations, there are some things you need to consider before you actually go out and get the product.

The first thing is to assess the computer-accommodation requirements. This involves consulting with the individual who has the functional limitation. Keep in mind that a computer accommodation comes in a group of one. We could have two people standing here, myself and another totally blind person, and one might be able to use synthetic speech whereas the other person might not. You might have two people with low vision with the same diagnosis from their doctor but one cannot see a visually enhanced system, while the other can. Therefore, computer accommodations have to be individualized as much as possible. Talk with the individual involved, get him/her involved from the very beginning. In addition include someone with technical knowledge about the capabilities of computers in the discussion. In the rehabilitation situation, the rehabilitation counselor should be involved. In an employment situation the employee's supervisor or manager should be involved.

The tasks that the individual is required to perform with the computer need to be considered. What are the future tasks of the employee going to be once the computer is on board? Finally, you need to find something on the market that will give you an optimum system which will eliminate or vastly reduce the functional limitation and permit the person to access the computer. There are various products on the market that will do this. I am amazed at what is being done in the research and development stages today. We are almost to the point now where we have computers that will actually pick up thought control and process it. Just a few years ago, you could not speak to a computer and have it understand "trained words." Today you can speak to a computer and it can process what you say. These are expensive systems, but it can be done. I have actually spoken to a system I did not train, and the system understood me.

When you are ready to view the computer systems that are available on the market, meet with various vendors of equipment, and arrange for a demonstration. The reason you need to have them actually show you what their equipment can do is because some vendors are unscrupulous. Many are very honest, but others will tell you anything as long as they think the check will be in the mail for the product.

One must consider what the best solutions may be to meet an individual student's and/or employee's needs. Likewise it is essential to meet the needs of specific employer and educational system needs at various levels (the university, college, or high school). Training is an important aspect of computer accommodation because if the person does not know how to use the equipment it will never be beneficial to him or her. Therefore, it is crucial that the individual receives the right kind of training when he/she gets the equipment so that the best use is made of the equipment and access systems.

Accommodations that are available for employees with visual impairments, include the glare protection and magnification screens. A glare protection screen can really help to reduce eye strain, whereas, the magnification screen enlarges the print one to two and one-half times normal. Magnification screens can also be helpful to those people who have some reduction in vision but have not been diagnosed as legally blind. In instances where a magnification screen is unavailable the text can be enlarged through the use of a copy machine. Many individuals can read such enlarged print while they may not be able to read normal-sized print. Print can also be enlarged through computer adaptations.

There are a number of useful devices for people who are blind. These include the following:

1. Hardcopy braille embossers which can be connected to a computer and which can output information in braille so the person can have access to text.

2. Refreshable-braille systems which have small strips of braille at the top.

3. Calculators that have braille dots in a 20-to-80-character display.

4. Synthetic-speech systems like the Braille 'N Speak that I use.

5. Systems which can be attached to a computer that output the information in synthetic speech as well as recite the information that is being inputted on the keyboard.

6. Optical Character Readers, which let you scan text into computer format and put it on disk which can be given to a person who does not see, and they can use their access system to read that text. Optical Character Readers are helpful in the office environment in general, and can also be used to help the visually impaired and other people who have print disabilities.

With regard to employees who are hearing impaired, training considerations are very important. If you make use of an interpreter service, for example, it is important to ensure that the interpreters are familiar with computer terms. If a person with a hearing impairment is taking a computer class, it is important to ensure that he/she is getting an accurate interpretation. In addition, class notes should be shared with the student who is hearing impaired because he/she cannot both look at the interpreter and take notes at the same time. Captioned training videotapes can be utilized so that the person who cannot hear can see what is being said on the video. It is also helpful to use a computer system that has a blinking error message instead of one that beeps. The blinking message will be more noticeable to the person who is hearing impaired. Telephone amplifiers are being used everywhere today; they are portable therefore can be moved from place-to-place, for easy use by people with limited hearing. Electronic Mail is a facility that moves mail around without using paper. Instead of being in paper form, it comes up on a terminal screen. People with hearing impairments can use this system very effectively without installing any kind of modification. Telecommunication Devices for the Deaf (TDD's) are very helpful for phone communication between a person with a hearing impairment and another person. If you need to speak with someone who is hearing impaired, you can contact the Federal Relay Exchange operated by the General Services Administration. The voice number is (202) 377-9555, and the TDD number is (202) 566-2673. They have operators who can take in information from a TDD and speak it out to the hearing person on the other end of the line. They then transfer the information coming from the hearing person to the TDD which will be displayed to the person with the hearing impairment. All conversations are confidential.

There are many keyboard alternative input devices for people who are motor impaired, These devices include the following:

1. Morse Code

2. Speech recognition systems

3. Optical Head Pointer Systems whereby you have a pointer attached to headgear, and you enter text to the system by moving your head around a screen with specialized keyboard software. You can also retrieve text with this type of system.

4. Eyegaze Systems with modified keyboards whereby you blink at the letter you want entered into the system.

5. Keyboard enhancement programs which will take some of these two and three-key sequence commands and lock them so the person can enter all three keys without the computer misinterpreting the command.

6. Macro facilities that turn many keystrokes into one keystroke to enhance the text that is entered into the computer and make the process simpler.

7. A "mouse" which is very helpful to a person with motor impairments. Other input devices include scanners, mouthsticks, headsticks and a variety of switches which can be connected to a functioning muscle to permit keyboard entry and retrieval of text.

The Department of Veterans Affairs has a Microcomputer Training Program for Persons with Disabilities. Listed below are a number of additional resources which may also be helpful. For information call Pat Sheehan at (202) 233-5525. Other training resources include: The Easter Seals Foundation. They have training and offer financial assistance for equipment. Contact Mr. Ed Porter at (312) 243-8400, Extension 195. The United Cerebral Palsy Association also has a number of training centers that they are establishing, and they offer financial assistance in getting equipment. Contact Mr. John Stroman at: (202) 842-1266. Regarding training for people who are visually impaired in the DC area, contact Mr. Joe Roeder PC Partners, Inc. in Baltimore, MD at: (301) 744-3724. Persons with all types of disabilities including the hearing impaired, contact Brennan Associates at: (301) 243-8010. They have very competitive prices and interpreters are included in course costs for the hearing impaired. Information about computer accommodations for the visually impaired, can be obtained from Mr. Elliot Schreier at the American Foundation for the Blind, National Technology Center at: (212) 620-2082.

Financing this technology is still a big problem as some of it is still rather expensive. The book "Financing Adaptive Technology" is available for $23.00 from Smiling Interface, Post Office Box 2792, Church Street Station, New York, NY 10008-2792; Telephone: (212) 222-0312.

In the federal sector, the General Services Administration's Clearinghouse on Computer Accommodations provides assistance with needs assessments and product literature regarding adaptive technologies. Contact Miss Susan Brummel at (202) 501-4926. Regarding resources for computer accommodations in the private sector, contact the IBM National Support Center for Persons with Disabilities in Atlanta, Georgia at (800) 426-2133. Also, contact the Job Accommodation Network (part of the President's Committee on Employment of People with Disabilities) and speak with Mr. Larry Fontan on (800) 523-7234. He knows adaptive products very well and will be happy to give you assessment information or literature.

INFORMATION TECHNOLOGY PROGRAM FOR PERSONS WITH DISABILITIES

PATRICK SHEEHAN
DEPARTMENT OF VETERANS AFFAIRS

Abstract

This article focuses on the Information Technology Center. This center, which is a part of the Federal Government, provides a program for people with disabilities within the Federal Government. Supportive services include training relative to the use of equipment so that individuals with disabilities can compete with colleagues. This training also serves as a mechanism for building self-confidence in the participants. In addition, the Center is also available to individuals with disabilities who are employed by private industry. In many cases, employees of the Center provide services at various sites in an effort to work with individuals with disabilities.

The program offered by the Information Technology Center is set up for people with disabilities within the Federal Government. These persons are offered training in the use of adaptive equipment, whether it is synthetic-speech or large-print systems like the TSI systems or some type of text-enlarging system. We train them to use these types of equipment, and to become familiar with what they will and will not do. We also offer training in basic computer technology from ground zero. This training includes computer capabilities, its components, and other relevant areas. We also offer courses in DOS and any application program that an individual might like to learn (dBase, LOTUS 1-2-3, Wordperfect, etc.). We try to get individuals up to speed by working one-on-one with them. After gaining confidence in their specific field, whether it is word processing or LOTUS, they are able to compete with their sighted colleagues and feel positive about what they can do with the computer.

Our procedure in working with individuals with disabilities involves visiting their work place. We work with them on their own system to enable them to gain confidence with their computer as opposed to visiting the Information Technology Center at the VA and dealing with an unfamiliar computer keyboard or network system. My forte is in large-print systems. I use one system at the VA, but have access to about three other systems. I have interfaced those systems with speech, and am very pleased with the results.

Individuals who are not working with the Federal Government, are also offered the resources at the Information Technology Center. Center services are relevant since they provide training which can be used on a daily basis. We are familiar with what works, what does not work, what is difficult to use, and what is user friendly. When individuals call the VA, I provide them with information about a particular piece of equipment, the way in which it works, whether or not it does a satisfactory job, and whether it should be recommended for use in specific situations.

We also have product vendors demonstrate the latest adaptive products and systems at the Information Technology Center, so that we can evaluate new products to be used by people who are blind or visually impaired at our Prosthetics Assessment and Information Center.

Solutions can be varied. One individual may like a particular type of synthetic speech. In my case, a certain large-print system may work fine while for another individual it may not work. The solutions are designed to meet individual needs. We invite individuals to come to our center to seek out techical assistance to satisfy their specific needs. It is felt that this is one of our most valuable services, bearing in mind we are not trying to sell any equipment, therefore, we will tell you the tradeoffs between systems. Another important part of our program is that we stress low-cost computer solutions. In many cases a top-of-the-line system is not what is needed to get someone up and running with a PC. We feel it is best to give a person the technology he/she needs to do his/her job. After they have had experience using PC technology and they access equipment for six months, they are in a better position to upgrade the computer capabilities since they will know what they need to complete their work tasks.

Both Federal Government and private-sector employers tend to get the access equipment, but are not provided with adequate training on how to use the equipment or software. Management seem to feel that the individual should be able to do the job with the equipment alone. They forget that they are always sending their nondisabled employees to training. It is important to let the individual who will be using the equipment choose what he or she needs to best meet his/her needs. My wife is blind, and I can tell you from experience that once an individual has chosen the access system and speech synthesizer he or she likes, you are not going to persuade him or her to change it. You had better not touch their equipment because they are totally in love with the stuff.

I have known a lot of people with disabilities who, once they have been shown how to use off-the-shelf applications with their access systems (and have worked with LOTUS 1-2-3 or Wordperfect), are just as capable and dynamic as anyone who uses that computer system. They have the desire to use the system and make it work for them. As mentioned above, we do evaluations of new technology for low vision and print handicapped areas. We try to keep up with what is coming out in the disability field in general, and we try to obtain the technology so we can examine it and let people know what we have discovered. We feel that communication between our staff and our clients is most important. Individuals gain independence by combining our input with their experience. A particular person is then able to determine what type of system will best work for him/her. In this way, the individual will better adjust to equipment he/she has had input toward selecting.

SECTION 1V

FUTURE FRONTIERS

ADVANCING FRONTIERS THROUGH COLLABORATION

BRIDGES TO LEADERSHIP 2000:
HOWARD UNIVERSITY YOUTH LEADERSHIP PROGRAM

SYLVIA WALKER AND SATWANT KAUR
HOWARD UNIVERSITY

Abstract

This article discusses the Bridges to Leadership 2000 program. The purpose of this program is to implement a service delivery model for the economically disadvantaged and minority youth with disabilities (ages 11-21). This program receives support from a wide cross-section of individuals and organizations. In Washington, D.C. youth leadership meetings take place on the first Friday of every month; special events are organized on several Saturdays during the project year. The program provides knowledge about the world of work, self-confidence and social skills. Various activities include children with disabilities as well as those without disabilities. The project is being carried out in the District of Columbia, New Jersey, Michigan, Georgia, New York, and California. A Career Day Conference and a Special Achievement Incentives Contest are implemented on an annual basis in participating cities.

PURPOSE

The purpose of Bridges to Leadership 2000 Program is to implement a service delivery model for economically disadvantaged and minority youth with disabilities. This unique program provides role models, mentorship, and work orientation that enables the participants to increase their social and work related skills. The program also facilitates their functioning at the post secondary educational level and in competitive employment. The training project offers experiences for young people and their families. These experiences are designed to bring about increased confidence, information about the world of work and positive self-concepts. Activities are designed for the economically disadvantaged and minority youth with disabilities between the ages of 11 - 21 in the Washington, DC Metropolitan area, New Jersey, Detroit, Atlanta, New York, Los Angeles, and other geographical areas in the United States.

The motto for the Bridges to Leadership 2000 Program is:

B uilding Bridges to
R ole Models
I ndependence
D ignity
G rowth
E conomic Excellence
S uccess

Program Description

The Youth Leadership Training Program was initiated in August, 1989. In order to implement this program, several schools and agencies in the Washington, DC area were contacted. Information flyers, membership and consent forms were developed and distributed to all participating schools and agencies in all geographical locations. This program is being conducted with the help of Howard University Research and Training Center for Access To Rehabilitation and Economic Opportunity (HURTC's) Task Force Committee in each of these locations. This program receives support from a wide cross-section of individuals and organizations. The following organizations have cooperated with the Center in the implementation of the Howard University Youth Leadership Training Program:

1. National Aeronautic and Space Association

2. American Association for the Advancement of Science

3. Howard University Office of Recruitment

4. The President's Committee on Employment of People with Disabilities

5. Pack 304, Club Scouts of the Boy Scout of America, Benjamin Banneker District of the National Capital Area

6. Youth Missionary Organization of First Baptist Church

Youth leadership meetings take place on the first Friday of every month. During each project year a number of special events are organized on Saturdays in Washington, D.C. These special events accommodate students who are unable to join the group during their regular monthly meeting, including children of members of the Center's Parents' Advisory Committee.

At the first meeting students selected team leaders and team names. This, for most students, was the first opportunity to work with a group in a democratic manner. Job training for youth with disabilities, in many cases, has been too narrowly focused with emphasis on specific job skills. Many training programs fail to focus adequately on the development of social communication and independent living skills (Walker, 1991). In addition, youth with disabilities are often steered towards positions where supervisors and co-workers are inadequately prepared to work with an individual who has a disability. All too often students with disabilities are encouraged to enter low level jobs such as mail rooms, food service operations and factories.

91

Youth with disabilities need to be prepared for work in a wide array of occupations including science, technology, human services, education, law, and allied health fields (Walker and Asbury, 1990). The Howard University Youth Leadership Training Program provides knowledge about the world of work, self-confidence, and social skills which are not readily available to the youth through typical job training programs. The Bridges to Leadership 2000 Youth Training Program offers information about non-traditional jobs for youth such as careers in Law, Education, Science, and Technology.

The seven teams from the Washington, DC area are:

Barnard Achievers
Ballou Knights
Nalle Positive Plus
Blacks with Abilities
Blacks On the Rise
Calvin Colts
Mighty Achievers

With the exception of the Mighty Achievers which meet bimonthly, these teams participate in the monthly meetings which focus on various career opportunities and educational requirements. Each team is given a monthly assignment in advance and is asked to then work within their school to develop print and audio-visual materials. Each team is asked to include the following types of information during their presentation:

1. Educational qualifications needed to pursue a specific career (e.g. Law, Education, Science, and Technology)
2. Investigate their own career goals
3. Specific job responsibilities
4. Accomplishments of minority professionals in the field.

The above guidelines provide a framework for specific team assignments. Team presentations are made in the form of short story, skit, or panel presentations. Guest speakers are invited to serve as role models and leadership partners. Guest speakers may or may not have disabilities but must be very successful people in their field. During their presentations, they share personal experiences including the types of barriers they had to overcome in order to achieve their professional goals.

Other special features of the Bridges to Leadership 2000 Program include:

The integration of disabled and non-disabled students: For example, non-disabled students and Pack 304 Club Scouts of First Baptist Church participate in field trips and special programs. In addition, each of the monthly meetings include both students with and without disabilities.

- **The Annual Career Day Conference and special seminars:** An Annual Career Conference is held which provides workshops, exhibits, and training materials for participants. In addition to the Career Day Conference which is held in Washington, DC, seminars and awards programs have been held in a number of cities including New York, Detroit, Atlanta, and Los Angeles.

- **Special Achievement Incentives contest titled, "Embracing Diversity:"** This is implemented on an annual basis. The contest which is held in a number of cities (Washington, D.C., Los Angeles, Detroit, Atlanta, and Newark) encourages students to express their creative abilities in the areas of art, creative writing, and three dimensional design. Prizes, awards and certificates are awarded based on specified criteria. Every student who enters, receives some type of recognition. Therefore this program provides positive reinforcement.

- **Networking and Collaboration:** The Howard University Youth Training Program relies heavily on collaborative efforts. In addition to Task Force Committees in each of the cooperating cities, the following types of organizations support the program: churches, corporate sector, public schools, and government agencies.

- **System Success Program, New Jersey Bell:** The "Systems Success Program," which is part of the Newark Board of Education in New Jersey, is a program which focuses on providing support and encouragement to high school students with disabilities. The HURTC is collaborating with the "Systems Success Program". Mr. Isaac Hopkins, a prominent community leader in New Jersey and a member of the HURTC's National Advisory Committee, provides a bridge between Howard University and the Systems Success mentorship program. Students and parents participate in Bridges to Leadership 2000 activities on an ongoing basis. For example, Systems Success students have participated in:

  A. The Embracing Diversity Contest
  B. Career Day Conference activities
  C. The 1990 National Symposium: Minority Americans with Disabilities

The latter was a part of the Annual Meeting of the President's Committee on Employment of People with Disabilities. These activities expose youth with disabilities to various social situations which in turn increase their social and communication skills.

Summer Employment Efforts

Bridges to Leadership 2000 also helps youth in finding summer employment. Various government and private agencies are contacted in order to identify possible job opportunities. Youth are assisted in completing employment applications (SF-171) and follow through with agencies. Summer employment information flyers are distributed, along with information sharing at various meetings including the Parents Advisory Committee meeting. A select number of students have also had opportunities to work at the HURTC during the summer. Students were made aware of the summer employment opportunities at the National Institute of Health and the Naval Research Laboratory. Information about job opportunities at various organizations and agencies is distributed during each project year.

References

Walker, S. (1991). Building bridges to employment for minority students with disabilities. OSERS News in Print, 3(4), 6-9.

Walker, S., and Asbury, C.A. (Eds.). (1990). Partnerships and linkages for success: Enhancing the employment potential of persons with disabilities. Los Angeles: The California Governor's Committee for Employment of Disabled Persons.

MAXIMIZING POTENTIAL: THE PARENTS' ROLE

SHIRLEY POINDEXTER DYER
CHAIRPERSON FOR THE PARENT ADVISORY COMMITTEE
HOWARD UNIVERSITY

Abstract

This article presents the importance of coping with a child's disability from a parental perspective. A major emphasis is placed upon motivating and discovering the child's potential. These goals are reached through the parent's direct interaction with the child and the teacher. Maximizing the child's potential includes taking an active role in the child's activities and achievements. This can be done by assisting him/her to assimilate into society and encouraging his/her language development. A note book of the child's progress is especially helpful. Finally, it is the parents responsibility to educate and sensitize the public about the needs of children with disabilities. School age children, physicians, and the general public should be educated about the abilities and needs of this population. This knowledge could be helpful to all who are involved with children who have disabilities.

PERSONAL STATEMENT

Aside from my involvement with the Center for the Study of Handicapped Children and Youth, I am also an employee of Howard University, in the Center for Academic Reinforcement where I serve as Administrative Assistant. I am the mother of a child with special needs because of a disability called "Autism." I also have a normal child. Both children live with my husband and me, and we are a very close family. I am happy to share with you today my views of the "special" parents' role in maximizing the potential of their children. Personally, I feel that it is primarily the parents' responsibility to do so, but I also realize that it is not an easy task.

Introductory Statement:

First, I want to express how utterly necessary it is for parents to accept that a child born with, or who later acquires a disability, is DIFFERENT. If we can do this we have surmounted the first, and the greatest hurdle (Beste, 1986; Bonnett, 1986).

Secondly, DISCOVER this different human being. By this, I mean, try to learn something about the way this person thinks, rather than impose your ideas and values. Not even normal children react positively to the "teeth-pulling" method. They withdraw. Your special child may withdraw completely, or mirror your chaotic emotions, or react obliviously with little interest in the environment.

You cannot effectively motivate a child to reach his or her fullest potential unless you do these two things first. In short, accept the difference and discover the child. Without these basic elements, you're working from an artificial basis bound for failure. Who suffers? Both parents and child suffer.

Some of us might think we are being noble, investing in persons with special needs, but in truth, we need them to invest in us. We need them to reach out to us in whatever way possible before we can really help. How? How do we do this? My son said it best. He told me that parents need to be "A lighthouse in the fog." "A thick branch over the quicksand." We must pull from ourselves our strongest talents, and sell our children an appealing image; a secure image; a rock. Make them want to invest in us and buy into us; show them there is something outside of themselves to latch onto; let them know that they are our most important commodities. This spells LOVE, and CARING in capital letters, and children, special or not, recognize and understand it. I know from personal experience that they will invest in it, and can be motivated to do things that some think should be impossible.

The Parent

As a parent, I have found it necessary to STOP, LOOK and LISTEN. It is part of discovering the child. STOP thinking about learning, playing, working, communicating and other social functions in a conventional way. LOOK at the child's behavior in an analytical way, but do not try to make judgements about it. Get guidance from school or other professionals if necessary, but also use that special parent's intuition born in each of us. LISTEN to everything the child says or does not say (Smith, 1980).

There is so much involved in "maximizing" the potential of a child with special needs. For example, a parent must learn when not to say NO to such a child. You might say NO to a normal child who yells in a grocery store, but when your special child yells out APPLE for the first time-- even in a crowded store, you DO NOT SAY NO! You clap your hands! The light bulb just turned on for that child, and he is reaching out to you--the "lighthouse in the fog"--for acceptance.

Aside from direct interaction with the child, a parent can help maximize a child's potential through parent/teacher interaction. Keep a tab on what's going on at school. The child could be a completely different person there, or may be having difficulties that even the teaching staff do not understand. Make sure the teaching staff receives information about the child's behavior at home. For instance, I have been told repeatedly over the years that my daughter cannot initiate conversation. In fact, she never stops talking at home, and even insists on having her time to talk about subjects she emphatically states are important for me to listen to. I tape some of these conversations and send them to school. The school also provides a notebook which we use daily to record home and school events and behavior. A notebook can also serve as a good chronicle of a child's progress.

Public Awareness

Public awareness, or the lack of it, is one of the most inhibiting factors in maximizing the potential of our special children. Some people seem to feel that anyone who is different is crazy. Some outwardly display their fear, their disgust, or wonderment as to why such people should be in public places. I call it the "Them and Us Syndrome." The only ones who seem to be purely receptive are the little children. But even they lose this quality when they grow up. The onus is on parents, in whatever small way possible, to educate the public. We owe it not only to our children, but to society. Anyone, everyone has the potential to become a person with special needs. It is possible that a family member, or friend, or co-worker, will be a special needs person in each of our lives. Why the "Them and Us?" "Them" could become "Us" at any given moment in time.

Some special parents get very angry when people ask questions about or stare at their children. An appeal is needed to help parents realize that these people are victims of a society that is ignorant about handicapping conditions and how families are affected. Some of these questions and stares really deserve a response, because the people truly want to understand, but may not know how to tactfully present themselves. You will readily know the ones who do not deserve a response. Conferences like this one are excellent vehicles for educating the public one-on-one. It is very important and nothing can take the place of it. Sensitivity and sensibility are two concepts that the general public could develop.

97

Since handicapping conditions are so prevalent in our world, it is recommended that such conditions be defined at the grade-school level (Scheifer and Klein, 1986). These children have the first encounters with special needs children, and should have the opportunity to understand how "they" fit into society with "us." Many of these children are the siblings of special needs children and have to live with the stigma imposed by the community. No one should think that because a person is in a wheelchair that the person cannot talk--but some do. Everyone should know how loving a Downs Syndrome child can be--but many do not. Everyone should understand basic facts about retardation--but they really don't.

Many physicians are not prepared to assist parents in this regard. My daughter's first pediatrician was not. When I asked questions, he wanted to know if we were having marital problems. I have heard similar accounts from a number of other parents. Many teachers do not read background information about special children, and may be ignorant as to how to help them without parent intervention (Wing, 1985; Scheifer and Klein, 1986). We, all of us, are just recently learning. What makes us think our professionals came up differently. They are just learning also, and unless they have special needs children themselves, we parents know a bit more about the basic concerns involved.

My Child

Finally, I want to tell a little bit about my personal situation. As I mentioned, I am the mother of a special needs child. My daughter is autistic--residual type. She started out being diagnosed as simply autistic when she was around three years old. She did not display human warmth, had no eye-contact, displayed ritualistic behavior such as rocking, finger flexing, handshaking, headshaking, belching noises, and a number of other such repetitive self-stimulatory acts over the years--one immediately following the other. She also would not communicate. I say "would not" because it was apparent that she had the capability but would not use it. She <u>looked</u> at our dog, and <u>talked</u> to him in what seemed to me a normal way. She looked at herself in mirrors and smiled and made faces. But with us it was like she was deaf and blind. She had perfect diction and repeated in echolalia style everything said to her, verbatim. She did not respond to pain, odors, and loud noises. However, there were certain noises that did bother her like the shaking of liquids and

98

crying babies. When she heard these, she could be upset for two hours or more. She used the toilet for the first time when she was four years old.

My daughter is now sixteen years old. She talks, reads, writes, is good academically in school--though not up to grade level. She retains information, practices excellent personal hygiene without my assistance, and is gradually integrating her ways of doing things in a normal way. These behaviors are consistent with those identified by Brutten (*cf.,* Brutten, et al., 1973). She is still very concrete in her thinking and somewhat bizarre in her habits, but assimilating into everyday life.

Our outlook for the future? I have no reason to believe that my daughter will not go on to higher education some day. She will have her first real job during the summer through the Mayor's Summer Youth Program.

How did we accomplish this? Basically by doing the same things described previously. Of course, each child will bring with him different qualities, and variations in methods (Wing, 1985).

My daughter would not come to us so we went to her. We got to know her, and to interact with her. I began doing what she did, whether it was to rock back and forth, scream or handshake. These were her first social interactions, and she began to RESPOND by REJECTING me. LISTEN TO THE MAGIC! She rejected me. That was a wonderful and appropriate response. My whole family joined in this concept, and over the years we have conquered each one of her self-stimulatory acts. For the first time in her life, I have not noticed a self-stimulatory sound or movement for several months.

If you have seen the movie "Son Rise" you saw a glimpse of what happened in my household. When I saw that movie I cried because it was the same approach I had used with my daughter. The only thing I did not like about that movie was that someone could get the impression that wealth is needed in order to work like that with a child. Both parents in the movie left work and stayed home for a year, I believe working around the clock with their child--rocking, twirling, or whatever he did. How many could afford to stop working? Well, my daughter is living proof that the same thing can be done in normal everyday activities--at home, in the car, walking along, everywhere. Amazing, our interaction was the very thing that made my daughter abandon each of these bizarre acts. She was desperately seeking to be alone--to do something that only she could do. I hope she has given up.

Language developed very similarly. I noticed that there was a pattern--a thin ribbon strung through everything that said "Reverse Me." My daughter started out with echolalia. She said her first sentence before she was a year old which was : "See the little flowers." I did not realize that she was echoing what she had heard me say the day before. I also didn't realize later on that she was attempting to reverse the echolalia. (Wing, 1985)

The day I realized that she wanted me to repeat--verbatim--everything she said, or seemed to ask, was the first day that she went to the bathroom with no prompting. She had said, "You go to bathroom." She was so emphatic that I had to look. She was almost bent over. My light bulb went on. For the first time I realized she wanted me to repeat what she said. She went. She went by herself. From that moment, I was echolalic (reverse echolalia, if that is a word). She told me what to say to her, what to ask her, how to play with her--everything. I used that medium to teach her proper behavior, vocabulary, social skills, and to discover her, the person. Soon I was able to get her to turn it around and initiate what she wanted to say or do without going through me. If I had only learned to STOP, LOOK AND LISTEN much earlier, she certainly would have been toilet trained before she was four years old (Wing, 1985).

How do we maximize potential? Since each special child is different from one another, there is no cut and dry method. In my opinion the mold is created by the child. There need only be receptive family members and teachers, and if one can access this mold--discover the real person in this child, then it can be used for retraining, and helping the child to reach his or her full potential. The poem below summarizes some of my feelings and thoughts regarding this.

THE INTRUDER

by SHIRLEY POINDEXTER DYER

A Child
A strange child,
In a world all her own, but
Which she did not make,

She rocked,
And she twirled,
She screamed in her room,
But She did not awake.

Dare I preside
In those unmindful eyes
And try to be a friend?

The end result
Would no doubt tell
Whether bending her will
Would make her well.

So I rocked with her
And twirled with her
And I too
Screamed in her room.

She tended not my eye,
And she did not like my play;
She turned from me in silence,
But I saw it this way:

By her attempt to exclude
My efforts to intrude,
The first contact was made,
Meaning she was now awake.

The end result
Was a great beginning
For a "special" girl
In a "special world."

References

Beste, P. (April, 1986). Are we exceptional parents? The exceptional child. 16(2), 49-50.

Bonnett, C. (July, 1986). Parenting the special child: How difficult is it? The Exceptional Parent. 16(7), 50-52.

Brutten, M., Richardson, S., and Mangel, C. (1973). Something's wrong with my child. New York: Harcort, Brace & Jovanovich.

Schiefer, M.J., and Klein, S.D. (Eds.). (1986). The disabled child and the family: An exceptional parent reader. Boston, MA: The Exceptional Parent Press.

Smith, S.L. (1980). No easy answers: The learning disabled child at home and at school. New York: Bantam.

Wing, L. (1985). Autistic children: A guide for parents and professionals. New York: Brunner/Mazel, Inc.

AMERICA'S MEAN STREETS:
A CHALLENGE TO YOUTH

ISAAC W. HOPKINS
NEW JERSEY BELL

Abstract

While America has made great progress in the removal of obstacles to productivity for its citizens with disabilities, a large segment of the society has been overlooked. Other groups who have been excluded include young people in inner city settings and the economically disadvantaged. This article focuses on the fact that crime and poverty are the worlds in which many of our African American, Hispanic, and other minority youth with disabilities must live and survive. The author challenges persons with disabilities, political leaders, and service providers to develop creative strategies to more effectively deal with the challenges which are cited.

This country has made great progress in removing obstacles to productivity for its citizens with disabilities. The Americans with Disabilities Act of 1990 is a triumph, not because it prepares persons with disabilities for the world of work, but because it prepares employers for persons with disabilities. ADA is a significant first step on a journey that must continue.

America needs to attack the disability issue on a totally different front--the prevention front. Many disabilities are preventable. Acts of violence and inadequate health care disable thousands of innocent people every year in the mean streets of our cities; the majority of the victims are African Americans.

For decades, Americans have heard tale after horrible tale about the living conditions for African Americans, Hispanics and other minority groups in our cities. Poverty, drug trafficking, violent crimes and the decay of the family unit have exacted a heavy toll on society. For the most part, these ills block the enormous social contributions which African Americans and other minority groups could be making now and in the future.

There has been no shortage of political rhetoric, noble intentions, nor even noble deeds aimed at cleaning up the wretched conditions in which African American and low income people live. Nevertheless, the situation worsens everyday. One cannot fault the leaders in the federal government, Congress and other public and private organizations who realize the simple fact that many persons in the African American and Hispanic communities are at a disadvantage. Many government leaders do not understand the magnitude of this disadvantage. There seems to be a mentality among them that the community itself is largely to blame and that it can pull itself up by the bootstraps.

True, humanity has an amazing ability to overcome adversity; an ability that can be likened to salmon swimming upstream against swift river currents. However, African Americans and other minority groups are often faced with grave situations, more like salmon trying to swim up Niagara Falls. The barriers are virtually insurmountable without the aid of the rest of the society and they are the product of a relentless chain reaction rooted in large part in poverty and neglect.

Under these conditions in the streets of America, survival--not success--becomes the objective. For many, life is a constant struggle to end each day alive and unhurt. Crime may be prevalent everywhere, but in the minority communities, it is frequently accompanied by violence. Ultimately, violence results in disabilities that render victims easy prey for subsequent attacks.

At Harlem Hospital, I became acquainted with a patient named Joe whose arm had been shot off in a petty robbery. The next time I saw him, his leg had been shot off. He did not seem to feel a bit sorry for himself. Losing limbs and becoming disabled to Joe is part of the only life he knows. Since many of his peers have had similar experiences, Joe is by no means extraordinary. Patients like him are commonplace in inner-city hospitals across the country.

Violence is one reason the percentage of citizens with disabilities is significantly higher among African Americans than in the general population. Another reason is inadequate preventive health care. Diabetes, for example, frequently leads to blindness and amputation. It is most prevalent among African Americans because second opinions and health maintenance instruction are largely unavailable in minority communities.

In a couple of ways, I suppose Joe could be considered lucky. He could have been killed just as easily as disabled--any day of the week. African American males between the ages of 15 and 24 are more than six times as likely to die from homicide or police intervention than their White counterparts. Even African American babies under a year old are almost twice as likely to be killed as White males between ages 15 and 41 (Johnson, 1988).

Given the high rate of infant mortality in African American communities, many of Joe's peers do not survive long enough to make it to the mean streets. In Harlem, for example, the mortality rate is higher than in crowded, famished, Bangladesh. Inadequate health care certainly has a role, but so does the drug culture. At the University of Medicine and Dentistry in Newark, New Jersey (which serves a predominantly African American urban area), 52 percent of the babies are born to substance-abusing mothers.

Further testimony to the prevalence of intravenous drug abuse is the fact that 25 percent of the babies at the university hospital are born to HIV-positive mothers--women who are at least carriers of the AIDS virus. AIDS is a leading cause of death in the African American community, especially among women.

It should be considered that when people with disabilities enter the rehabilitation system (hit the comeback trail), they need optimism, cheerfulness, and spirit--by the ton. Under the above described conditions, it is hard to imagine anyone being able to sustain the positive attitude necessary to complete the journey back to productivity.

Unfortunately, there is more cause for pessimism and mental distress. Negative attitudes emerge early in the lives of urban children. The children of people like Joe realize that they have very little chance of a better life. Like Joe, many of them have no idea that a better life even exists.

One explanation is that these kids have no role models to represent successful life. Parents of many African American youngsters aren't around their children long enough to be effective role models. Less than 42 percent of Black children live in homes with two parents. Most of the time, the father is absent. Much of the time, the father is in jail. Although African American males between the ages of 15 and 35 make up only 2 percent of the U.S. population, they account for 47 percent of prison inmates. In New Jersey state prisons, that 2 percent produces no less than 70 percent of those behind bars. Because African American males, ages 15 through 35, are the most reproductive segment of the population (Johnson, 1988), the result of sending them to jail, is that the greatest number of children at risk of educational and economic failure are left without a father.

It saddens me to visit a school and to look at the faces of a room full of bright youngsters, knowing all the while that their innocence soon may be history--that their intelligence is likely to be wasted. The realization of such possibilities causes the cycle of poverty and crime to be sustained.

It is a vicious cycle that swallows whole communities. Few inner-city citizens escape its grip. What is worse is that this is the world in which many of our African Americans with disabilities must live and get around. Considering the prosperity of its society as a whole, America should be ashamed of this situation.

Awareness is our first line of defense. First, youth with disabilities in our community must be made aware of the risks and dangers in the streets of our cities. Their disabilities may not repel violent crime; on the contrary, they often attract criminals.

Second, youth with disabilities should be made more aware of positive role models --people who have overcome both their disabilities and the wretchedness of the mean streets (Walker, et al, 1988). Last spring, a group of Newark high school students with disabilities accompanied me to Howard University's Research and Training Center for Access to Rehabilitation and Economic Opportunity and to the Conference of the President's Committee on the Employment of People with Disabilities. While in Washington, these teenagers were exposed to something they had seen little of --success.

They were infused with optimism and inspired to achieve. It was seen in their faces.

Finally, we must enhance awareness among our political leaders--both federal and state. They already are aware of urban problems, but many are totally misguided as to the causes. Inner-city squalor, crime, violence and the drug culture do not result from "bad genes" or "bad culture;" they result from unrelenting forces set in motion by poverty and kept in motion by society's continued neglect. Like fish attempting to swim up waterfalls, Americans who are subjected to these forces inevitably wind up at the bottom.

References

Johnson, J. (1988). The endangered Black male/ The "New Bald Eagle" community planning perspectives. Silver Spring, MD: Management Plus Consulting and Training Services.

Walker, S., Fowler, J.W., Nicholls, R.W., and Turner, K.A. (Eds.). (1988). Building bridges to independence: Employment successes, problems and needs of Black Americans with disabilities. Washington, D.C.: President's Committee on Employment of People With Disabilities.

COLLABORATIVE MODELS: PARTNERSHIPS FOR SUCCESS

JOYCE KEENER
MICHIGAN REHABILITATION SERVICES

Abstract

This article explores the lack of effective rehabilitation programs for minority persons with disabilities. The author proposes non-traditional methods and approaches for implementing and enhancing services for this population. Professionals are encouraged to challenge the system by providing leadership and the commitment to make change. Emphasis is placed on creative approaches in response to the unique needs of minority Americans with disabilities.

Research conducted by Howard University and others has shown that minority persons with disabilities fall far below the success ratios compared with non-minorities in rehabilitation programs (Atkins, 1988; Bowe, 1985; Walker, 1988). In fact, statistics indicate that traditional and ordinary programming is not sufficient in meeting the needs of minority persons with disabilities. There are a myriad of rationales for the lack of employment successes, several of which have been highlighted in studies conducted at Howard University (Walker, Fowler, Nicholls and Banner, 1986; Walker, et. al, 1988).

A number of compounding variables interact to reduce the rehabilitation success of non-white persons with disabilities. These include: low socioeconomic status, lack of educational opportunities, and poor health care (Thornhill and Torres 1988; Walker, 1986). Non-traditional methodology and different approaches are required to ensure that minority persons with disabilities needs are met, and that skills, abilities and equal employment opportunities are achieved.

Inclusion, education and employment opportunities must be the operative words used as we embark on future frontiers. The collaborative model may be one such frontier by which change may be affected for minority persons with disabilities (Walker, 1989; Asbury and Walker, 1989).

Many persons are aware of the adage -- "if it doesn't fit, don't force it." Minority persons with disabilities do not necessarily "fit" in traditional programs and we have tried continually to force a fit (Walker, 1988). Some would challenge that the "system" has been in place for years, and therefore, something elsewhere must be wrong. My answer to this challenge would be: Yes. The

Detroit-Windsor Bridge and the Washington Monument have also been in place for a long time, but this is not to say that repairs, changes or a little fixing up periodically are not necessary for future longevity of service.

The Collaborative Model approach provides for the establishment, development, and linkages of people with a common cause or goal (Walker, 1989). The following explanation will provide information about the manner in which the Collaborative Model is filling the gaps for a system badly in need of repairs. The discussion which follows, provides an overview of various components of the Collaborative Model and ways in which it may enhance the rehabilitation system.

Collaborative Approach: Non-Traditional

I. Bringing Different Groups Together

Allows the diverse members of the group to learn that they are not isolated in their problems and concerns; there is nothing to fear from other groups that represent minority persons. We are more alike than different. Outcomes are:

o   The elimination of fear.
o   The sharing of common goals

II. Understanding

There is an opportunity to gain a personal understanding of our common needs, problems, and concerns; to do an assessment of our previewed differences so that we may begin to move forward.

III. Communication

The lack of communication is perhaps the biggest obstacle to overcome in addressing sensitive and diverse issues. Good communication between group members is essential in that it is the forum by which cultural practices, issues, needs, and barriers may be discussed. Through communication, information about new and existing minority organizations may surface. Communication also provides global (national) knowledge and information that sometimes are only shared between certain cultural groups, but have significance to other minority communities. Clear lines of expectations may be established through communication.

IV. Broad Spectrum Models

The Collaborative Model process can be a tremendous voice in determining what commitments are made and to whom. We all have heard or seen the E.F. Hutton commercials -- which say in essence, that when they speak, people listen. When collaborative models are established throughout rehabilitation communities, they may be known by various names, but their main thrust and purpose will be singular. I make the analogy of Beatrice Company -- you may not know the company's name, but you are very familiar with their products.

V. Career Opportunities

The realization is that low-paying jobs for minority persons with disabilities will only reinforce substandard living, health care, and educational pursuits. If an individual has a career and a skill, he/she is not limited to one certain part of this country. A job should be only the means by which one begins preparation toward a career. In most instances, a career affords the individual a decent and livable wage. We must provide the leadership, the voice, and make the commitment to effect change.

Future

We must continue to network within our own states, but also with other states and minority groups on a national basis, via conferences, newsletters, etc. Information and communication are vital. Minorities groups have been studied and researched continually and the statistics for the most part have changed significantly in past years. (Atkins, 1986; Walker, 1988). What we must now do is utilize some of this research for the betterment of minority disabled persons. Here, at Howard University Research and Training Center, there is a large amount of quality research available. This information must be put in the hands of our minority leaders at local and national levels. We must hold them accountable for their actions or lack of actions. The needs of minority persons with disabilities must not be lumped together geographically or otherwise. If this is allowed to happen, various groups will be overlooked and their specific needs will not be addressed.

Finally, the future of the Collaborative Model must stress that the goals for minorities are for the benefit of all. We cannot combat the powers that be if we operate in a separatist fashion; nor can we get into the crabology mode. For example, if you place crabs in a barrel, they will pull the others back in order to get out of the barrel first. I wish to leave you with this thought:

"People will doubt what you say, but.. Believe what you do!"

References

Asbury, C.A., and Walker, S. (Eds.) (1989). Partnerships and linkages for success: Enhancing employment potential for persons with disabilities. Los Angeles: The California Governor's Committee for Employment of Disabled Persons.

Atkins, B.J. (1986). Innovative approaches and research in addressing the needs of nonwhite disabled persons. In S.Walker, J.W. Fowler, R.W. Nicholls, and K.A. Turner (Eds.). Equal to the challenge: Perspectives, problems, and strategies in the rehabilitation of the nonwhite disabled. Washington, D.C.: Bureau of Educational Research, Howard University.

Walker, S., Belgrave, F.Z., Banner, A.M., and Nicholls, R.W. (Eds.). (1986). Equal to the challenge: Perspectives, problems, and strategies in the rehabilitation of the nonwhite disabled. Washington, D.C.: Bureau of Educational Research, Howard University.

Walker, S., Fowler, J.W., Nicholls, R.W., and Turner, K.A. (Eds.) (1988). Building bridges to independence: Employment successes, problems and needs of Black Americans with disabilities. Washington, D.C.: President's Committee on Employment of People with Disabilities.

Walker, S. (October - November, 1989). _The collaborative model: Building bridges to employment_. The President's Committee on Employment of People with Disabilities.

Walker, S. (1991). Building bridges to employment for minority students with disabilities. _OSERS News In Print_, _3_(4), 6-9.

EMPOWERING MINORITY PERSONS WITH DISABILITIES THROUGH COLLABORATION

TONI KILLINGS
COMMISSION FOR RACIAL JUSTICE
UNITED CHURCH OF CHRIST

Abstract

This article presents an overview of the partnership between the Commission for Racial Justice of the United Church of Christ and the Howard University Research and Training Center. The organizations are collaborating to promote success and employment of minority persons with disabilities. The purpose of this collaborative effort is to develop resources, sponsor conferences, and symposia in order to enhance public education and advocacy concerning the Americans with Disabilities Act.

INTRODUCTION

The African American church has historically been at the forefront concerning various issues such as marshalling the efforts of people to dismantle the strongholds of racism and discrimination in America. Although little emphasis has been attributed to the church and its efforts on behalf of people with disabilities, monumental contributions are springing forth. As pastors and parishioners become conceptually knowledgeable of the plight of minority persons with disabilities, the needs of this population can be met (i.e. accessibility, counseling, etc.). Ideally, actions taken by the church should motivate businesses and agencies to react in a similar fashion.

The collaboration of the church with social agencies and educational centers has proven to be beneficial to people with disabilities. The United Church of Christ has collaborated with the Howard University Research and Training Center in order to promote partnerships between the African American Church and educational centers.

The Commission for Racial Justice

As I reflect on our theme for the Conference--"Future Frontiers in the Employment of Minority Persons with Disabilities"--and for this season--"Collaborative Models: Partnerships for Success," I am heartened by the positive and optimistic outlook and tone of leaders like Dr. Sylvia Walker and her staff. I am also encouraged by the concept of the "half full glass"--rather than "half empty"--that permeates the philosophies for success presented here at the Conference.

"Collaboration" will probably be the key approach for effective implementation of many projects of the future. As the collaborative model is being launched, it is expected that the relationship between the United Church of Christ Commission for Racial Justice and the Research and Training Center at Howard University will be mutually beneficial.

The Commission's goal is a "justice project" to initiate and develop a national network and program of action that will effectively challenge racial discrimination directed toward persons with disabilities. Sadly, racism is alive and well in the church--though fortunately, not unchallenged.

The United Church of Christ has more than 2,000 churches--each of which will be solicited for involvement in this effort. The approval and cooperation of each pastor will be sought. It is also hoped, in addition, that these pastors will enlist the assistance of various individuals and groups. The first step will be the establishment of a task force.

Additionally, assistance will be requested from other ecumenical groups, as well as various national bodies of the United Church of Christ. These will include: the Network of Persons with Disabilities, the Board of Homeland Ministries, the Office for Church in Society, the Office of Communications, the Council for Health and Human Service Ministries, and other ecumenical bodies. Theologically, Christian organizations are called to affirm the equal value of all human beings without regard for race or ability. The issue of racism and persons with disabilities is an issue that the Church should confront in the interest of human equality and social justice (Wells and Banner, 1986).

For the Commission, it is a matter of adding a new dimension to the racial justice struggle which has been waged for more than 25 years. In the global community, racism continues to be a determining factor that contributes to the oppression and exploitation of millions of persons. Most notably is the racist apartheid regime of South Africa. Last year, as part of the "hands on" policy of the Commission, many Angolans came to this country to be the specific guests of the Commission and our Executive Director. This was not a social visit. The Angolans were amputees who had been "land mine" victims of the political unrest in that country. More importantly--they were children of God who were given a chance to once again be ambulatory. They received medical

111

care, and Christian love, while being fitted for prostheses in this country. Christian agencies should continue to stand ready to be used as God's instruments wherever and whenever the challenges arise.

As the Collaborative Model is developed, research will focus on the following:

o   Social (and other) demographics related to ethnic persons with disabilities;

o   Compiling resources and other educational materials to widely distribute throughout the ecumenical network;

o   Sponsoring conferences and symposiums--particularly focusing upon the role of the church;

o   Enhancing public education and advocacy concerning the Americans with Disabilities Act;

o   Disseminating educational materials with emphasis on how racial and ethnic persons can effectively make use of important legislation;

o   Collaborating with national organizations concerned about the plight of persons with disabilities in order that the particular circumstances of racial and ethnic persons be highlighted, and promoting this issue as a major national justice issue.

All this will be patterned after the models heretofore used very successfully by the Commission in scores of projects throughout our 25 year history. These include:

o   The Special Higher Education Program,
o   Mentally Retarded Offender Advocacy,
o   New Approaches to the White Community,
o   Leadership Development & Training,
o   Economic Development,
o   United Church of Christ Constituency Development,
o   Economic Racial Justice,
o   Toxic Waste and Race,
o   Evaluation and Summary in book and video forms,
o   Funding by the United Church of Christ Neighbors in Need.

Reference

Wells, M., and Banner, A.M. (1986). The role of the Black church in advocating the disabled community. In S. Walker, et al. (Eds.), Equal to the challenge: Perspectives, problems, and strategies in the rehabilitation of the nonwhite disabled. Washington, D.C.: Bureau of Educational Research, Howard University.